CAMBRIDGE MUSIC HANDBOOKS

Mozart: The 'Haydn' Quartets

CAMBRIDGE MUSIC HANDBOOKS

GENERAL EDITOR   Julian Rushton

Published titles

Mozart: The 'Haydn' Quartets

John Irving

University of Bristol

PUBLISHED BY THE PRESS SYNDICATE OF THE UNIVERSITY OF CAMBRIDGE
The Pitt Building, Trumpington Street, Cambridge CB2 1RP, United Kingdom

CAMBRIDGE UNIVERSITY PRESS
The Edinburgh Building, Cambridge CB2 2RU, United Kingdom
40 West 20th Street, New York, NY 10011–4211, USA
10 Stamford Road, Oakleigh, Melbourne 3166, Australia

© Cambridge University Press 1998

First published 1998

Printed in the United Kingdom at the University Press, Cambridge

Typeset in Monotype Ehrhardt 10.5/13pt

A catalogue record for this book is available from the British Library

Library of Congress cataloguing in publication data
Irving, John.
Mozart: The 'Haydn' quartets / John Irving.
p. cm. – (Cambridge music handbooks)
Includes bibliographical references and index.
ISBN 0 521 58475 2 (hardback). – ISBN 0 521 58561 9 (paperback).
1. Mozart, Wolfgang Amadeus, 1756–1791. Quartets, strings.
Selections. I. Title. II. Series.
ML410.M9I73 1998
785'.7194'092–dc21 97–7268 CIP MN

ISBN 0 521 58475 2 hardback
ISBN 0 521 58561 9 paperback

AH

Contents

Contents

Acknowledgements

I am grateful to the staffs of the following libraries for access to manuscript or printed materials: the British Library, the Bodleian Library, Leeds Central Library, Sheffield University Library, Bristol University Library, Internationale Stiftung Mozarteum, Salzburg, Jagiellonian Library, Kraków. Thanks are due also to my parents for their encouragement at all stages of the project. I am grateful to the following for help and advice of various kinds: Cliff Eisen, Jim Samson, Wolf-Dieter Seiffert, Penny Souster and most especially to Julian Rushton for his many perceptive comments on the draft typescript.

Introduction

Mozart's six string quartets dedicated to Joseph Haydn (K.387, K.421, K.428, K.458, K.464, K.465) are established keystones of the chamber music repertoire and frequently feature in concert programmes, broadcasts and recordings by the most prestigious professional ensembles. While brief accounts of these quartets have previously appeared in articles and books over the years, reflecting the changing agendas of several generations of musicologists and speaking to a diversity of readerships, no single book exists devoted to these seminal works.[1]

The 'Haydn' set contains some of Mozart's most famous pieces (the 'Hunt' Quartet, K.458, and the 'Dissonance', K.465, for instance), works in which, according to Alfred Einstein, Mozart 'completely found himself ... music made of music'.[2] These works embrace some of his most memorable melodic writing, and some of his most refined compositional thinking, often animated by counterpoint. It is true that counterpoint had been an important factor in some of his earlier quartets (K.155–60 and K.168–73), but it is arguably a weakness there, rather than a strength, since no attempt is made to integrate the strictly fugal writing into the prevailing 'galant' environment of elegant melodies supported by simple harmonies within a symmetrical, even predictable, periodic framework. The result is a rather uncomfortable disjunction of different expressive types, representative of a real stylistic crisis during the early 1770s.

That crisis required for its resolution a new way of integrating the melodic and harmonic elements of the emerging classical style so that neither was a mere passive support for the other. While the solution was achieved largely through the technical requirements of opera (a genre to which both Mozart and Haydn devoted themselves with some

1

vigour during the 1770s), chamber music played a far from insignificant role. One of the triumphs of the classical string quartet was the provision of a texture in which counterpoint was fused with articulate melody resulting in that refined 'conversational' quality which is so prominent a feature of, for example, Haydn's Op. 33 quartets of 1781–2. The quartet was surely in some sense a metaphor of contemporary enlightenment ideals, as expressed in Rousseau's social contract (1762), balancing individual freedom with social responsibility and accountability.[3] Within Haydn's Op. 33 set the individual voice attains its authoritative identity as much by virtue of its interrelationships with the rest of the ensemble as by its individual thematic and rhythmic configurations. This was perhaps the 'new and special manner' to which Haydn drew the attention of potential subscribers to this now famous opus. In general as well as specific ways Haydn's new technique was to have its impact on the six quartets that Mozart was to dedicate to him in 1785.

In every bar of these pieces Mozart demonstrates complete mastery of the quartet idiom, both in his treatment of individual instruments and in the handling of textures. While there is no shortage of melody and accompaniment, in which the first violin takes the lead, there are many memorable solos for the other instruments. Among these are the prominent viola solo at bars 67–72 of the first movement of the very first quartet in the set, K.387 in G (which Mozart himself would have played in early performances of the piece), and the unforgettable intervention of the cello in its high register at bar 18 of K.458's Adagio. The range of textures is huge: full-blown fugato in the finale of K.387; octaves at bar 26 of K.428's slow movement; double octaves (with pizzicato support) at the end of the Trio of K.421; powerful unison writing in the Andante cantabile of K.387 (bars 29 and 85) and at the opening of K.465's Minuet. Melodic decoration, dialogue, contrast of high and low register, legato and staccato: there is scarcely a texture that is not found in this set.

Texts

The 'authentic' text of these six quartets is a difficult issue. The first edition (in separate playing parts) by Artaria (Vienna, 1785)[4] differs in a number of respects from Mozart's autograph 'score'. For instance, the 'Hunt' quartet, K.458 in B flat is placed fourth, whereas in the print it comes third;[5] there are also some discrepancies in the movement headings and tempo markings. The Minuet and Trio of both K.428 in E flat and K.465 in C are 'Allegro' in Mozart's autograph, but 'Allegretto' in the print; the finale of K.464 in A is given as 'Allegro' in the autograph: but as 'Allegro non troppo' in the first edition.

By far the largest quantity of divergent readings between the two sources concerns the placing or even the presence of articulation marks and bowings. There are literally hundreds of small variants. In the first movement of the D minor quartet K.421, for instance, the first edition is short on slurs, especially when compared to the autograph: it lacks a crescendo mark for the first violin in bar 105; three bars later the second violin has no trill over its last note and no tie over the barline into bar 109; in bar 110 this part lacks a staccato mark for the first crotchet; and so on. The articulation of the opening theme of K.464, on the other hand, is more consistent in the print than in the autograph. In the autograph the upbeat crotchet only rarely has a staccato mark (four appearances only, of which three are in the development section), whereas in the print the staccato appears much more frequently throughout the movement, though even here no consistent policy is detectable.

It could be argued that the first edition, which Mozart himself perhaps saw through the press, ought to take precedence over the autograph, in which there is substantial evidence of Mozart's reworking of some passages, including even the redrafting of the order in which the variations of K.464's slow movement appear. According to such an argument, the Artaria print of 1785 represents Mozart's 'final' text, a public statement dedicated, moreover, to Haydn, the foremost European composer of the age. Unfortunately, such a view is untenable. The Artaria text is so scrappy and inconsistent in detail that it cannot have had the composer's authority; it certainly is not an 'improvement' upon the composing score.[6] While neither autograph nor print presents a wholly accurate or consistent text the autograph at least has the merit that it derives directly from the composer, revealing clearly his struggles to work out difficult passages, that is, to discover the 'right notes'. In this sense it is a 'final' text. The *Neue Mozart Ausgabe* (*NMA*) wisely adopts the autograph as its copytext, except that it follows the printed order by placing K.458 in third place, amending its readings from time to time in accordance with the first edition where that preserves a superior text. While *NMA* clearly offers the best available scholarly text of the quartets, it is unlikely to be in many people's possession. Among the numerous reliable alternatives are the Dover reprint of Breitkopf and Härtel's 1881 edition,[7] the Eulenburg miniature score,[8] Einstein's 'authentic' edition[9] and the miniature scores published by Universal Edition, Philharmonia, Boosey & Hawkes and Kalmus.

1

Mozart's early quartets

Mozart's first string quartet, K.80 in G, was completed at an inn in the northern Italian village of Lodi on 15 March 1770, 'at 7 o'clock in the evening' according to an annotation on the autograph manuscript.[1] In a letter of 24 March 1778 Mozart reminded his father of the piece, and explained that he had arranged for copies of it to be made for Baron Otto Heinrich von Gemmingen-Homberg (1753–1836), a government official in Mannheim. Between 13 December 1769 and 28 March 1771 Mozart and his father were on tour in Italy. For Wolfgang this was a period of invaluable exposure to Italian operatic styles which bore fruit in commissions to compose two operas for Milan: *Mitridate, re di Ponto* (first performed on 26 December 1770) and the serenata, *Ascanio in Alba* (17 October 1771), to celebrate the marriage of Archduke Ferdinand. The Mozarts made a second journey (to supervise arrangements for *Ascanio*) between (mid?) August and 15 December 1771, and a third (24 October 1772 to 13 March 1773) to attend rehearsals for *Lucio Silla*.[2]

During these Italian visits Mozart encountered such diverse personalities as Giovanni Battista Sammartini (*c*. 1700–1775) and Padre Giovanni Battista Martini (1706–84), major figures in eighteenth-century Italian composition and musical theory. Leopold recalls a meeting with the former in a letter from Milan dated 10 February 1770: 'It would take too long to describe in detail the evidence of his knowledge which Wolfgang has given in the presence of Maestro Sammartini and a number of the most brilliant people, and of how he has amazed them'. Wolfgang's subsequent meeting in Bologna with Padre Martini, perhaps the foremost musical scholar of the eighteenth century, is described with considerable pride by Leopold in a further letter of 27 March:

[Wolfgang] has been most thoroughly tested, and the fact that Padre Martini, the idol of the Italians, speaks of him with great admiration and has himself set him all the tests, has increased his reputation all over Italy. We have visited him [Martini] twice and each time Wolfgang has worked out a fugue, for which the Padre had only written down with a few notes the *ducem* or *la guida*.

Wolfgang's musical prowess led to him being awarded two diplomas during his Italian journeys, from the Accademia Filarmonica in Bologna (1770) and the Accademia Filarmonica in Verona (1771).[3]

The six quartets K.155–60 also belong to the Italian years. All were composed in Milan in late 1772 and early 1773. On 28 October 1772 Leopold wrote to his wife from Bozen (Bolzano), noting that Mozart was writing a quartet (possibly K.155) 'to pass the time'; another letter, dated 6 February 1773, refers to the fact that Wolfgang was currently composing a quartet, possibly either K.157 or K.158. Unusually, this set of six quartets is arranged in a specific key-sequence, by falling fifths: D, G, C, F, B flat, E flat. Each is in three movements, the typical Italian practice in the early 1770s as seen in the works of, for instance, Sammartini. K.156, K.157, K.158 and K.159 each have highly expressive minor-key middle movements, all slow except for K.159, which is a remarkably passionate statement. In these works Mozart demonstrates an early mastery of the quartet idiom with passages of extended imitative counterpoint.

Mozart's seven earliest quartets betray their Italian influence, particularly in a tendency towards clear, transparent textures in which the two outer parts, treble and bass, carry the main burden of melodic and harmonic interest to which the inner parts provide a 'filling'. At times the polarity of treble and bass is reflected in the appearance of the extant autographs. In the opening Allegro of K.155 in D, Mozart's outer parts in the passage beginning at bar 33 are in a markedly different ink-shade from the second violin and viola, evidence that the inner parts, which provide a recurrent 'offbeat' quaver figure, strengthening the chordal harmony, were filled in at a later stage of composition, after the essential strands, theme and bass, had been determined.[4] Elsewhere, as at the beginning of this movement, the primary impulse was melodic, as may be seen from a careful examination of bars 4–12 of the autograph, in which the alignment of the first violin part against the supporting chords beneath strongly suggests that Mozart conceived (or at least, wrote down) the melody of this passage first, before returning to add the accompaniment.[5] Although such a melodically inspired compositional process was to remain with Mozart all his life, it reinforces in these quartets the centrality of theme in the definition of both texture and structure. In the opening Presto of K.156 the exposition is segmented into a succession of phrases each characterised by a new melody, and while the key-scheme is in sharp focus throughout it is the Presto's unfaltering melodic thread that provides real coherence. Typical 'fingerprints' of the Italian idiom include the repeated-note quaver bass-line (K.80/i, K.157/i, K.160/i), a feature that maps out a generally slow and uniform rate of harmonic change against which the primary melody stands out all the more clearly; modulation to the dominant (or 'secondary' dominant) by means of a prominent chromatic rising step in the bass just before the cadence (K.80/i, bars 7–8; K.155/i, bars 19–20; K.157/i, bars 29–30), a procedure associated with the repeated-note quaver bass patterns; cantabile melodies played in thirds (K.155/i, bars 64–7; K.157/i, opening; K.159/i, bars 4–6), and occasionally octaves (K.155/iii, opening); an engaging rhythmic verve, with pronounced variety of articulation (K.155/iii, opening; K.157/i, bars 31–8; K.160/i, bars 16–23 and 24–9); 'predictable' phrase extension by means of sequence, sometimes in a pattern akin to the falling suspension chain so familiar in the works of Corelli, Vivaldi and Sammartini (K.157/i, bars 109–16); and an almost unrelieved symmetry of phrasing in four- and eight-bar groups.

Mozart perhaps felt that something was lacking in the easy charm of this overtly optimistic, lightweight style. At any rate, there are some significant digressions into a more expressive vein, as, for instance, in the minor-key slow movements of K.156, K.157, K.158 and K.159. These exploit affective melodic writing, as in the Adagio of K.156, or the Andante of K.157, whose triadic opening theme soon takes on a chromatic twist, and powerful unison writing (K.157, bars 45–8, for instance). In the central G minor Allegro of K.159, Mozart achieves perhaps his most powerful statement in this set. Its broad expressive range incorporates a fusion of dynamic, sharply articulated and accentual figures (bars 1–12, 21, 36–57, 74–88) with contrasting legato themes (bars 13–20, 30–6, 57–66, 66–73, 89–108), along with a satisfying union of diatonic and chromatic tonal space. Stylistically, it sits somewhat uncomfortably with its more graceful Italianate neighbours. Along with the near-contemporary G minor Symphony K.183 it represents something of Mozart's darker side. It is certainly an impressive achievement for a seventeen-year-old.

Elsewhere in these early quartets, Mozart strikes the pose of the learned contrapuntist, perhaps as a concession towards equality of participation of all instruments in the polyphony and to offset the frequently unrewarding inner parts (especially the viola's). Fugatos occur in a variety of locations, usually timed to coincide with the arrival of a new section or key (K.80/i, bars 16 and 36; K.155/i, bar 54; K.156/i, bar 72; K.158/ii, opening). Finally, there is evidence that the composition of these quartets taught Mozart at least one valuable lesson about the importance of proportion in achieving the desired effect. His original E minor Adagio for the G major quartet, K.156,[6] was cancelled and replaced by a second attempt in the same key, tempo and time-signature, even featuring the same theme, but significantly diluting the prominence of diminished-seventh harmonies. Mozart's original version was saturated with this chord-type: he had employed it at the very opening to deflect the tonality to A minor, for instance, before continuing in the relative major, G. At this stage the diminished seventh is used too much for effect – an end in itself, rather than a means to an end; in the revision, appearances of this chord (at the end of the first phrase, reinforcing the tonic, E minor, for instance, and again at the beginning of the second section, in bar 15) serve a structural purpose, marking out important moments in the evolution of the movement and supporting its overall expressive purpose, rather than suffocating it.

Mozart's next six quartets, K.168–73, were composed only a few months after the completion of K.155–60, in Vienna during August and September 1773. Unfortunately no mention of their origin is made in Mozart's surviving letters from this time. Wolfgang Plath has proposed that the idea of a new set of quartets was Leopold's and that Wolfgang completed these pieces in order to satisfy his father's wishes. Clearly, a group of quartets would have been a useful and potentially marketable addition to the young composer's portfolio while in the Austrian capital, and it is quite plausible that Mozart senior was seeking preferment to a court chamber music appointment for his talented son by way of some novel quartets demonstrating a mastery of the traditional skills of counterpoint.

There is certainly much more fugal writing in these pieces than in K.155–60. Imitative counterpoint invades some sonata development sections, as at bars 42–50 of the opening Allegro of K.168 in F, or bars 37–57 of K.169 in A (a passage later featuring inversion of the theme). It is also found in the slow movement of K.171, the Minuet of K.172, and the finales of K.168 and K.173. There is an altogether more 'serious' attitude at work here, so pronounced as to imply an external, rather than internal, stylistic motivation, as if these works were intended as a kind of curriculum vitae. In the muted Andante of K.168 Mozart demonstrates his canonic skill in the best Fuxian mould – a craftsmanship that might commend itself equally to an imperial or ecclesiastical employer.

It is also notable that the finales of K.168 and K.173 are fully developed fugues, and not just fugatos within a sonata form. This fact further highlights the air of artificiality about these quartets and reinforces the argument for regarding them less as unified artistic statements than as a sales brochure. Seen in this light, the somewhat stilted chromatic fugue that ends the D minor quartet K.173 assumes the status of a demonstration – somewhat akin, perhaps, to an item from Bach's *Art of Fugue* – in which the manifold stretto entries of the theme during the course of the finale, occurring in a variety of temporal and intervallic positions, are to be 'read' both as evidence of the young composer's skill in handling the traditional contrapuntal forms so esteemed in Vienna, and as a deferential nod towards that tradition in which he sought employment.

Whatever their original motivation, these quartets were not subsequently issued until 1785 in manuscript copies by the publisher, Christoph Torricella – an event that caused something of a spat between Torricella and Artaria, who had just issued Mozart's 'Haydn' quartets.[7] Cliff Eisen has recently made an intriguing suggestion that the works may have been offered on subscription in Vienna in 1775.[8]

Many commentators have remarked on the influence of Haydn's quartets Opp. 17 and 20 on Mozart's six Viennese quartets. Einstein, for instance, takes this for granted: 'For the first time (in K.170) [Mozart] writes variations as a first movement, as Haydn did in Op.17 no.3; for the first time he too suddenly writes fugues as finales (K.168, 173) ... Involuntary reminiscences set in. The beginning of the first movement of K.168 is like an echo of Haydn's Op.17 no.3, in the same key; one of the fugue themes from Haydn's Op.20 no.5 returns in Mozart as an Andante (K.168).'[9] While K.168–73 seem on a superficial level to betray the influence of Haydn (most especially, perhaps, his Op. 20, composed the previous year), the link is not so straight-forward as it first seems: Haydn's Op. 20 'Divertimentos' (as they were entitled) were not published until 1774, and then not in Vienna, where Mozart might have known about them, but in Paris, by La Chevardière; they were published in a different edition by André in Offenbach-am-Main in 1775. If Mozart knew Haydn's quartets by mid-1773, he must have discovered them in (unauthorised) manu-script copies.[10]

For all that Mozart's style evolved towards a much more profound co-ordination of the elements of classical musical language during the 1770s and 1780s, his later quartets retain some vestige of the sunny elegance of the earliest quartets. The 2/4 finales of K.458, K.428 and K.465 recapture at times the innocence of those of K.155, K.157 and K.160, particularly in the phrasing and articulation of their themes, and the transparency of texture provided by use of dialogue (as, for example, at bars 49–64 of the finale of K.157: compare bars 16–30 of the finale of K.458). Likewise reminiscent of the early set are the occasional passages of octave writing, such as that found at bars 20–1 and 64–5 of the Minuet of K.428, while the expressive cantabile idiom of the Andante of K.465 recalls a similar sentiment to K.160's Un poco Adagio. What separates the later works from the earlier is a new-found integration of melodic accessibility and contrapuntal discipline within a flexible periodic framework. In K.155–60 Mozart's attempts to inject a unanimity of purpose into the quartet ensemble were lim-ited to the somewhat gratuitous importation of fugatos; for instance, bars 54–9 of K.155, which, while achieving their immediate aim of vertical integration, actually detract from the integrity of the unfold-ing horizontal structure by introducing too many uncomfortable lurches in texture back and forth between counterpoint and melody with chordal accompaniment.

By the time of the 'Haydn' quartets, Mozart was in complete control of the vertical and horizontal elements of texture and structure. One illustration of his greater maturity in the application of counterpoint for a structural purpose is seen in the finale of K.428 in E flat. At bar 43 Mozart introduces a striking dotted figure in high treble register, imitated one bar later at the seventh below by the second violin and supported by *forte* quaver chords. Later on (bar 186), Mozart builds upon this idea by adding a further strand of counterpoint (the viola entry in bar 189), generating the downward sequential extension of the harmonic pattern and turning this moment into a point of dramatic culmination. This is counterpoint in the service of structure, a device only imperfectly understood by the Mozart of K.155–60 and K.168–73, but gloriously revealed in these quartets for Joseph Haydn which occupied such a special place in Mozart's own affections.

2

Genesis of the 'Haydn' quartets

The earliest mention of these quartets comes in a letter Mozart wrote to the Parisian music publisher Jean Georges Sieber on 26 April 1783, in which Mozart tries to interest him in publishing the three piano concertos, K. 413–15, composed in 1782 and 1783. He also notes that he is

> not very well pleased, however, with the way in which works are engraved in Vienna[1] ... This is to inform you that I have three piano concertos ready, which can be performed with full orchestra, or with oboes and horns, or merely a quattro. Artaria wants to engrave them. But I give you, my old friend, the first refusal ... Since I wrote those piano concertos, I have been composing six quartets for two violins, viola and cello. If you would like to engrave these too, I will gladly let you have them. But I cannot allow these to go so cheaply; I mean, I cannot let you have these six quartets under 50 Louis d'or...

Mozart perhaps refers to Sieber as his 'old friend' because he had previously engraved the six violin sonatas K.301–6 in 1778 (for 30 Louis d'or).[2] The tone of the letter is familiar, and suggests that Mozart felt confident that his offer might be accepted. It wasn't. Both the concertos and the quartets subsequently appeared in engravings by Artaria, whose work he disparages to Sieber. This might be felt to be ironic, but, in fact, Mozart perhaps knew all along that, should Sieber refuse, Artaria was still waiting in the wings. The quartets appeared in print in about September 1785.

Actually, Mozart's letter to Sieber is a little economical with the truth, since by 26 April 1783 he had, in fact, completed only one of the six quartets, K. 387. Had Sieber immediately accepted Mozart's offer, there would have been a desperate struggle to complete the remaining five works. In the event, the sixth, K. 465, was not completed until 14 January 1785.

Traditional accounts of the quartets have tended to assume that they were written in two relatively short bursts of creative activity: K. 387, K.421 and K.428 between late December 1782 and July 1783, and K.458, K.464 and K.465 between November 1784 and January 1785. The manuscript of K.387 is dated 31 December 1782; K.458 was entered in Mozart's own handwritten thematic catalogue[3] on 9 November 1784, while K.464 and K.465 were entered on 10 and 14 January, respectively. That leaves K.421 and K.428, for whose dating we have no first-hand documentary evidence. There is an anecdote, reported by Constanze to Vincent and Mary Novello in 1829, that Mozart was working on the D minor quartet K.421 while she was in labour with their first child, Raimund, and therefore around 17 June 1783.[4] To judge from the evidence of the manuscript, K.428 also dates from about this time (see below).

It is not known at what stage Mozart decided to dedicate these pieces to Haydn, rather than to a member of the nobility who might have paid Mozart handsomely for them. Haydn's approval of K.387, K.421 and K.428 at a private performance on 15 January 1785 evidently provided some encouragement.[5] The following month (12 February) the remaining three quartets were played to him by Mozart, his father and the two barons Tinti. This is the occasion on which Haydn famously told Leopold 'Before God, and as an honest man I tell you that your son is the greatest composer known to me either in person or by name. He has taste, and, what is more, the most profound knowledge of composition.'[6] An alternative stimulus may have been the Op. 2 string quartets of Ignaz Pleyel (1757–1831) which had appeared in 1784, with a dedication to his teacher, Haydn. As pointed out by Marc Evan Bonds,[7] a dedication to Haydn, the most esteemed composer of the day, was in itself a good selling-point. Artaria made much of precisely this fact in the announcement of Mozart's newly published quartets that appeared in the *Wiener Zeitung* on 17 September 1785.[8] Mozart admired Pleyel's quartets, as noted in this letter to his father of 24 April 1784:

> I must tell you that some quartets have just appeared, composed by a certain Pleyel, a pupil of Joseph Haydn. If you do not know them, do

try to get hold of them; you will find them worth the trouble. They are very well written and most pleasing to listen to. You will see at once who was his master. Well, it will be a lucky day for music if Pleyel should be able to replace Haydn.[9]

The autograph

Mozart's autograph score of these six quartets is in the British Library, London.[10] It was among the manuscripts sold by Constanze Mozart to the publisher André.[11] Thereafter it was purchased by Johann Andreas Stumpff (the owner of a number of Mozart autographs, including that of the Fantasia and Sonata in C minor, K.475 & 457, now in the Mozarteum, Salzburg).[12] On Stumpff's death in 1847 the autograph of the 'Haydn' quartets was purchased by Charles H. Chichele Plowden. It subsequently passed to his daughter, Harriet Chichele Plowden, who bequeathed it to the British Museum in 1907. The manuscript comprises 68 leaves, of which 127 sides contain music. The paper, measuring roughly 31 or 32 cm × 22 or 23.5 cm, is ruled with twelve staves.

It is well known that, in the dedicatory preface to these quartets, Mozart described them as 'il frutto di una lungha, e laboriosa fatica'. Indeed, on examining the quartet autographs, one is struck by the sheer quantity of revision, both to immediate details of continuity and the drafting of larger paragraphs. Perhaps, then, Mozart's choice of words goes further than a customary dedication 'formula' in which one routinely began one's address with some posture of self-abasement, in this case, the difficulty with which Mozart had mastered a genre for which Haydn was already especially noted.[13] These quartets really did cost him a lot of time and trouble.

Mozart used no fewer than ten different types of paper in the autograph of these quartets and there are several 'overlaps' where the same paper-type occurs in different quartets. For instance, fol. 38 of the autograph, containing the last part of K.428's slow movement, consists of a single leaf which was once, according to Alan Tyson's exhaustive examination of the watermarks, part of the same sheet as fols. 14–15, containing the first movement of K.421 (June–July 1783). Perhaps, then, Mozart was working on these two quartets simultaneously? Fol. 10, another single leaf, containing a final revision to the intricate polyphony of bars 130–42 of the finale of K.387, was originally attached to fol. 22, on which is written the concluding bars of K.421. Evidently, then, this revision to K.387's polyphony postdates the supposed completion of that quartet (31 December 1782) by about six months.

More interesting still is the case of K.458. Its first movement is written on paper not found elsewhere in the 'Haydn' quartets, but identical to that on which Mozart wrote the beginning of the Horn Concerto in E flat K.417, the manuscript of which is dated 27 May 1783. Probably, then, the first movement of K.458 was begun around this time, more or less simultaneously with K.421 and K.428. Moreover, the varying ink-colour in the first movement of K.458 suggests that it was written in two distinct phases: bars 1–106; and bar 106 to the end. Assuming that bars 1–106 (consisting of the exposition and the opening section of the development) were begun in mid-1783, and given that roughly the second half of the movement was written on a different paper-type (also found in the first movement of K.464), it looks as if Mozart left this first movement in an incomplete state for some time, perhaps for more than a year: his 'Verzeichnüss' date of 9 November 1784 evidently refers only to the completion of this second phase of composition.[14] Given the coincidence of paper-types, it seems clear that Mozart was working on K.464 simultaneously with the second phase of K.458. The finale of K.464 and parts of K.465's first movement likewise share the same paper, suggesting that the composition of the last two quartets in the set also overlapped to some degree – a possibility strengthened by their respective dates in the 'Verzeichnüss' (10 and 14 January 1785).

Textual revisions

Within a study such as this it is impossible to go into comprehensive detail regarding Mozart's revisions to particular passages in the quartets. Fortunately for Mozart scholarship, the *Kritische Berichte* to the *NMA* volume of these six quartets has finally appeared, and those interested in pursuing further the minutiae of Mozart's composing and writing habits may profitably do so in that indispensable reference tool.[15] The most extensive revisions are found in K.387, K.458 and K.464, throwing some light on Mozart's compositional processes. The texts of K.421, K.428 and K.465, while not altogether 'clean' texts, offer less in the way of significant revisions and recastings.

Mozart clearly had problems with the polyphonic continuity in one passage of K.387's fugato finale. There are three draft versions of bars 125–42, the opening of the development section. In the familiar version Mozart divides the chromatic crotchet patterns in bars 129–42 between the viola and cello in what seems an obvious dialogue beneath a canonic semibreve duet in the violins. Actually, he only introduced this texture at a very late stage, some six months after the quartet was originally completed on 31 December 1782. In addition to the 'original' text at the bottom of fol. 11 and the top of fol. 11v. there are two cancelled drafts on fol. 13v in which he struggles to achieve consistent notation of this chromatic section in either flats or sharps and in which the precise disposition of the notes among the inner parts is rather different.[16] The final solution to this apparently knotty problem of notation and textural balance was written on the separate leaf of paper associated with the variations of K.421 (mentioned above, p. 15), dating from June–July 1783.

The autograph of K.464 reveals that Mozart recast the order of the Andante variations during the actual course of composition. On fol. 50v one finds the eventual variation 6 (featuring repeated staccato semiquavers in the cello) and on fol. 52 the *minore* variation 4. Originally Mozart had intended the section beginning at bar 126^2 to follow bar 72, and at that stage had not envisaged a minor-key variation. In the autograph, the numbering of the variations is altered to take account of the recasting.

Subsequent to the publication of the *NMA* text of K.464 an autograph bifolium containing two passages from a contrapuntal string quartet in A major has come to light in a private American collection. One, at least, of these relates to the finale of KV 464,[17] although neither sketch is preceded by clefs. In the second fragment Mozart experiments with a possible stretto outlay of the chromatic theme, similar in nature to the passage in the development beginning at bar 95, or else in the coda, from bar 229, to one of which passages it perhaps relates.

Ex. 2.1 Original opening of the finale of K.458

Mozart's first attempt at a finale for K.458 was a 65-bar Polonaise (K.589a; Anh.68) on the same paper-type as that quartet's Minuet and Trio (1783, perhaps by late July that year).[18] The first section (eight bars) is fully scored; thereafter, only the first violin is written out, though in fine detail, including copious articulation marks and with occasional cues for the supporting polyphony. At bar [65] the melody appears to be leading back into a reprise of the opening theme. However, Mozart never completed the movement, preferring instead a finale in duple rather than triple metre.

Intervening between this abandoned Polonaise and Mozart's eventual 2/4 finale is a cancelled thirteen-bar sketch (fol. 29v of the autograph). This is a Prestissimo *alla breve* beginning with the theme in double the familiar time-values and with the second violin and viola parts swapped (see Example 2.1). Starting at bar 5 of this version, Mozart's original plan was to introduce contrapuntal imitation of the theme at one bar's distance successively between first violin, second violin and viola, entering on B flat, E flat and F respectively. At bar 9 the tune is stated a third time, now accompanied by a running crotchet countersubject in the cello.

Between this cancelled draft and the eventual finale (from which the opening thematic imitation is removed) Mozart's strategy had shifted from a quasi-contrapuntal texture to one characterised instead by concertante interplay between 'solo' first-violin statements and 'tutti' interjections from the rest of the quartet, a texture that returns at various points. After the double-bar, however, there is a significant change of texture in favour of counterpoint. Most of the development is contrapuntally conceived, featuring imitative entries very similar to bars 5–9 of the cancelled draft. For example, the concertante dialogue of bars 143–8 is now an interlude between imitative successions (bars 140–3: second violin/viola; and bars 149–58: paired entries every two bars on first violin/second violin, second violin/viola, viola/cello, the latter pair repeated in sequence at bars 155 and 157). Further imitative overlaps occur at bars 169 (second violin, followed by first violin in bar 172), 183–5 (first violin/second violin/viola – the last in diminution) and 187–9 (second violin/viola/first violin – the last entry again in diminution). Mozart's eventual choice of finale represents a radical recasting of the nature of the movement, from a version in which 'learned' imitative counterpoint (stretto overlap, followed by theme and countersubject) acts as a defining characteristic from the outset (as in the finale of K.387) to one in which imitation serves a contrasting structural function, deliberately withheld until the central development so as to act as a dramatic interruption of the established pattern and revealing – in retrospect – that there is more to this apparently light-hearted contredanse than at first meets the eye.

3

Steps to publication

By 1785, Mozart was a commercial success. Publishers were keen to market his recent works, and even some older pieces written while he was still in the employ of the Salzburg archbishop. This enviable public status must have been especially gratifying to Leopold Mozart, who spent some ten weeks with his son in Vienna during the spring of 1785 attending concerts at which Wolfgang played his own compositions.[1] Leopold could not fail to have noticed the significant exposure his son's printed works were receiving in the Viennese press. During the period 11 February – 25 April 1785, when Leopold was in the capital, at least eight press announcements appeared advertising Mozart's works for sale, including the following placed by Artaria, announcing the three Piano Concertos, K.413–15:

> At the art establishment of Artaria Comp … three Pianoforte Concertos by Herr Kapellmeister Mozart, in A maj., F maj., and C, have been engraved, and each is to be had at 2 fl. 30 kr.[2]

Also issued during Leopold's stay in Vienna was a keyboard arrangement of items from *Die Entführung aus dem Serail*, available in manuscript copy from the Court Theatre copyist Wenzel Sukowaty for 15 fl. (advertised in the *Wiener Zeitung* on 16 April),[3] and from the copyist and music-distributor, Lorenz Lausch, who published an itemised list of numbers from *Die Entführung* and prices in the *Provinzialnachrichten Wien* the following week. Leopold refers to the published piano version of the opera in his letter to Nannerl Mozart of 12 March:

> As for the clavier arrangement of 'Die Entführung aus dem Serail', all that I can tell you is that a certain Torricella is engraving it. Your brother is arranging it, but it isn't quite finished yet. He may have only

completed Act I. I shall find out. Torricella has also engraved three sonatas, only one of which has a violin accompaniment.[4] Well, I shall buy everything that has been published...

During the course of the same year further Viennese newspaper advertisements announced the availability in either print or manuscript of Mozart's cantata *Die Maurerfreude*, K.471, completed on 20 April that year;[5] the much older Divertimento K.247 for two horns and solo strings (composed in 1776);[6] and an assemblage of pieces offered by the important Viennese music dealer Johann Traeg (1747–1805), who frequently offered manuscript copies of Mozart's work for sale during the 1780s. His advertisement in the *Wiener Zeitung* on 14 September 1785 offered K.247 (again), possibly K.413 and K.414 (though they are described as 'double concertos'), the G major Piano Concerto K.453 ('N.B. quite new'), the Trio in B flat K.254, 'Various new Symphonies' (?), and three sets of keyboard variations, K.455 (1784), and K.359 and K.360, for violin and piano, composed four years previously.[7]

Something of the zeal with which publishers sought Mozart's works at this time is captured in this 1785 prospectus issued by Torricella, announcing the publication of some variation sets for piano (probably K.265, K.398 and K.455):

> The eagerness with which the works of this famous master are on all sides especially awaited (these works win the attention of the connoisseur with their exceptional art and freshness, and so gently move our hearts with their melodies) persuaded me to make these very beautiful variations my own and thereby be once again of service to the most esteemed lovers of music.[8]

Among Viennese music publishers of this time, Artaria was pre-eminent.[9] The Artaria family was of Italian descent and, before moving to Vienna to trade as art dealers in 1767, had worked in Mainz. In the Austrian capital the firm's trading activities expanded into maps and music. Artaria's first musical publication was issued in 1778, some eighteen months after they had begun selling music. Within a few years Artaria was to become the most prestigious of Viennese music publishers and was associated with some of the most important composers, including Haydn, whom they first published in 1780, Mozart, whose violin sonatas K.296 and K.376–80 were issued in November 1781, and subsequently Beethoven.[10]

By 1785, Mozart was a commercial 'hot property' for Artaria. In that year they published not only the 'Haydn' quartets (in September) but the 'Haffner' Symphony, K.385, and the C minor Fantasia and Sonata, K. 475 & 457, dedicated to Thérèse von Trattner, advertised in the *Wiener Zeitung* (Artaria's usual means of drawing attention to new music available from his outlet on the Kohlmarkt) on 7 December 1785.

The 'Haydn' quartets were published early in September 1785. The dedication to Haydn is dated 1 September and copies of the playing parts were on sale soon afterwards. The title-page reads as follows:

SEI

QUARTETTI

PER DUE VIOLINI, VIOLA, E VIOLONCELLO

Composti e Dedicati

al Signor

GIUSEPPI HAYDN

Maestro di Capella di S.A.

il Principe d'Esterhazy &&

Dal Suo Amico

W.A. MOZART

Opera X

In Vienna presso Artaria Comp.

Mercanti ed Editori di Stampe Musica

e Carte Geographiche.

As mentioned in Chapter 2, Mozart had initially approached the Parisian music publisher Sieber about these pieces, though unsuccessfully, for Sieber never published the quartets during Mozart's lifetime: evidently he preferred the chamber works of J. C. Bach, Dittersdorf, Holzbauer and Vanhal, popular composers whose works were advertised again and again in Parisian catalogues at this time.[11] Artaria, on the other hand, was extremely interested in Mozart's most recent work. On 17 September 1785 the following announcement was made in the *Wiener Zeitung*:

At the art establishment of *Artaria Comp.* ... are to be had: By Herr Kapellmeister W. A. Mozart, six entirely new Quartets for two violins, viola and violoncello, *Opus* X, engraved, for 6fl. 30kr. – Mozart's works call for no special praise, so that it should be quite superfluous to go into details; it need only be affirmed that here is a masterpiece. This may be taken as the more certain since the author has dedicated this work to his friend Joseph Haydn, Kapellmeister to Prince Esterházy, who has honoured it with all the approval of which a man of great genius is alone worthy. In view thereof the publishers have not spared any costs either to present amateurs and connoisseurs with this work beautifully and clearly engraved as regards both paper and print, relying upon it that the price fixed for it, which could not have been less than 12 fl. for manuscript, will not be regarded as excessive, since the Quartets cover 150 pages.[12]

One week earlier, Artaria's rival, Torricella, had placed the following advertisement in the same journal:

Six Quartets for two violins, viola and violoncello, are to be had from my art establishment in the Kohlmarkt ...[13]

These were not the same quartets, however, but K.168–73, composed in 1773. Artaria and Mozart were immediately stung into action by what they saw as a piece of sharp practice by Torricella, whom they no doubt thought was attempting to cash in on the arrival of the new 'Haydn' quartets by having others (carefully unspecified) by Mozart ready for sale simultaneously. Mozart (presumably instructed by Artaria) placed a notice accusing Torricella of attempting to deceive the public into buying these older quartets in mistake for the new ones:

As the art dealer Herr *Torricella* also announced six Quartets by Mozart at a low price in the recent newspapers, without saying whether they were in manuscript or engraved, old or new, Herr Mozart regards it as his duty to inform the estimable public that the said six Quartets are by no means new, but an old work written by him as long as fifteen years ago, so that amateurs who had been expecting the new ones should not be wrongly served...[14]

Torricella, incensed by this slur on his professional integrity, replied as follows:

Since in the announcement of Herr Artaria Comp., concerning the publication of the latest and newest Quartets, it has been quite superfluously asserted that those which I made known to the public had been written fifteen years ago, and the public thus seemed to be warned against a kind of deliberate exploitation, I find myself under the necessity of explaining that my not saying whether they were engraved or in manuscript, old or new, should in fact prove that I had no intention of misleading the public – supposing that proven honesty should fail to speak for me.

As regards the fifteen-year-old Quartets, then, I believe that they too stand in need of no other recommendation than their master's name – indeed, I am convinced that they too may be a novelty for many an admirer of the latest, thanks to their quite peculiar quality; and that therefore amateurs could never be wrongly served, since these too are assuredly Mozart's children...[15]

At this point the dispute appears to have rested. No further correspondence on the matter appeared in the *Wiener Zeitung*, though Artaria continued thereafter to place announcements in the press advertising Mozart's 'new' quartets, for example on 18 October in the *Wiener Realzeitung*:

By Herr Kapellmeister Mozart, six new Quartets for two violins, viola and violoncello, *Opus* X. 6 fl. 30 kr. At Artaria's on the Kohlmarkt...[16]

While no account of the financial success of Mozart's 'Opus X' survives, there is some circumstantial evidence that they did not sell especially well, at least not for their original publisher. Artaria was still advertising the works in the Dessau *Neue Litteratur und Völkerkunde* in March–April 1787 (along with Mozart's symphonies, piano concertos, piano sonatas, piano and violin sonatas and duet sonatas), indicating that significant copies remained in stock two years after the first printing. In August the same year Dittersdorf wrote to Artaria in terms implying that his own quartets ought to sell rather better than Mozart's because they were written in a more accessible style.[17] Numerous reprints of the quartets made in Vienna, Paris, London, Leipzig, Offenbach and Cologne were issued over the next thirty or forty years, each of which further diminished Artaria's longer-term profits. Leopold Mozart owned a copy of the original Artaria edition from which he 'work[ed] carefully through three of the new quartets with [Anton] Preymann ... until 8 o'clock. We can now perform them some time, as I shall coach two people in the second violin and cello parts, and play the viola myself...'[18]

4

The individual quartets: a synopsis

The following account is intended to provide an overview, guiding the reader through each of the six 'Haydn' quartets. It concentrates principally on describing the forms of individual movements, defining the main moments of structural articulation, principal themes, keys, textures and other salient features. This is not intended as a comprehensive account; inevitably, some movements are treated at rather greater length than others. No musical examples are given; access to a score is assumed throughout.

Two issues require consideration at the outset: thematic terminology in sonata form, and octave registers within recapitulations. The arguably anachronistic terms 'first subject' and 'second subject' are applied in the following discussions of sonata-form movements. Whether conceptually 'right' or 'wrong', these terms have undoubtedly attained 'conventional' status and are widely understood. Of course, such terminology only developed during the nineteenth and twentieth centuries and would not have formed part of Mozart's technical vocabulary, for all that it has pervaded much subsequent writing on his music. This is not the place to enter into a discussion of the eighteenth-century theoretical alternatives (which actually confuse more than they clarify).[1] Provided that they are not understood too literally, the terms 'first subject' and 'second subject' do not unduly confuse or falsify Mozart's sonata structures. Radical departures from the familiar 'textbook' procedures in any case receive special note in the synopsis.

The octave register within which the second-subject group is recapitulated is by no means standard in the quartets, nor was any prescription for deciding upon a 'correct' octave register given in contemporary theoretical literature. In fact, Mozart never recapitulates the second-subject material consistently either a fourth higher or a fifth lower in these quartets, but normally migrates between the two registers.[2] His procedure in the first movement sonata-form allegros is as follows:

K.387: initially fourth above (bar 133), subsequently fifth below (bar 145).

K.421: initially sixth above (bar 94 – tonic minor reprise of material originally sounded in the relative major), subsequently third below (bar 102).

K.458: mostly fourth above (bars 153–4, continuing as far as bar 205), thereafter fifth below (bar 206).

K.428: initially fourth above (bar 138), subsequently fifth below (bar 152).

K.464: initially fifth below (bar 198), continuing fourth above on decorated repetition of the second subject (bar 206).

K.465: initially fourth above (bar 191), subsequently fifth below (bar 211), but later returning to fourth above (bar 218).

In the following synopsis of each movement, therefore, the statement that a recapitulation is 'regular' (implying that a recapitulation broadly follows the plan of the exposition, bringing back the exposition's secondary-key material within the tonic) does not mean, of course, that it transposes the exposition up or down in its entirety.

K.387 in G

(1) Allegro vivace assai

The exposition begins with a ten-bar period whose main theme provides an early foretaste of the element of chromaticism that is to become such an important feature of the quartet as a whole. The theme is immediately repeated within a more imitative contrapuntal framework (bars 11–24), introducing fragmentation of the main material from bars 1 and 2 (the first violin's chromatic quavers in bar 2 are passed between both violins in bars 13 and 14, for instance), a longer chromatic line sweeping through all four parts (from bar 16), and a decisive modulation to a dominant-seventh chord on A in preparation for the D major second subject (bar 25). The second-theme group, like the first, depends upon upbeat scansion and large-scale repetition of paragraphs (bars 25–30, 30–8), but while the first-subject group can be seen to evolve from a small number of closely-knit motifs sounded in the first few bars, the second group is thematically much more diverse, incorporating a wide range of rhythmic variety between successive patterns at bars 39, 42, 49^4 and 54. (Incidentally, bars 53 and 54 were an afterthought – Mozart's exposition originally ended at bar 53 with the *pianissimo* cadence on D.)

The development (one of the most expansive in any of these six quartets and subdivided by two prominent recurrences of the closing exposition figure at bars 88 and 99) commences with declamatory references to the main theme (bars 56, 61, 68), but much of it consists of material not directly related to the exposition. Bars 70–80 are exclusively concerned with periodic sequential presentations of a new idea arising in the viola solo and moving through a succession of seventh chords on C, A, D and B (the dominant of E minor), although a brief reminiscence of bars 52–3 occurs at bars 86–7. Following the first main punctuation is yet more new material (bar 90) and a further repeat of bars 52–3. The development's final stage (retransition) is characterised by fragmentation of the exposition's closing trill motif, which loosens into even semiquavers in bar 104 over a pedal D, giving way in bar 108 to a wholly regular recapitulation, with dominant-key material duly transposed back into the tonic, G, and following the original sequence of events with only minor modifications, such as the expansion of the semiquaver passage beginning at bar 38 of the exposition into a more powerful tonic statement at bars 146–55.

The overwhelming impression of this movement is one of elegant symmetry. Its engaging ebb and flow is produced not by an endless succession of predictable four-bar periods, however, but by a subtle mixture of smaller and larger units. A particularly good illustration of the great flexibility of Mozart's phrasing is found at the opening of the development section: the momentum of bars 56–60, based on the main theme, is skilfully checked through its five bars in contrast to the much more animated character of the exposition.

Periodicity, clearly a crucial issue in later eighteenth-century musical language, was discussed in great detail by the theorist Joseph

Riepel, one of whose treatises was owned, as noted previously, by Leopold Mozart and which, therefore, may have been used by him in the musical instruction of his son.[3] Riepel's preference was for symmetrical, balanced phrases in units of two or four bars. His discussion hinges on cadential articulation of phrases, especially on tonic (*Grundabsatz*) and dominant (*Quintabsatz*) degrees, indicating tonic or dominant termination, respectively, with black or white squares above the phrase-ends of his examples. Riepel explains subdivision of a phrase (2 + 2 bars, 4 + 4 bars, and so on, including irregular subdivisions such as 3 + 2 bars), and he also discusses the symmetrical balance of phrases to form larger continuities, such as the construction of Mozart's second subject here (bars 24^4–30 being repeated at bars 30^4–36). He goes on to explain some methods of transforming phrases by means of repetition (perhaps in sequence) of an initial or internal figure, by expansion of the end of a phrase, or else by reiteration of the cadence for extra emphasis.[4] Examples of sequential internal repetition and cadential reiteration are found in K.387's ten-bar opening theme. Its sections (*Einschnitten*) consist of a two-bar phrase ending on the supertonic chord; a balancing phrase returning to the tonic (what Riepel terms a *Grundabsatz*); a one-bar phrase; an immediate repetition; another (varied) repetition and 'weak' termination on the submediant (bar 8); and finally a varied repetition of bars 7 and 8 concluding on the tonic degree (bar 10).

(2) Menuetto and Trio. Allegro

Mozart's spacious Minuet is a miniature sonata form. Its 'first-subject group' extends to bar 20, incorporating a segmented main theme (bars 1–10), the second of whose components is a prominently accented solo chromatic line, alternating *piano* and *forte* dynamics.[5] This is immediately turned upside-down in the cello at bar 7 before the whole of the opening phrase is repeated with light melodic decoration and with a new sequential countertheme against the chromatic scale (bars 14–15, 16). Bars 17–20 form a modulating transition to the dominant of the dominant, heralding the entry of the second subject in bar 21. A secondary thematic idea ensues at bar 28^3, before the 'exposition' closes in D major with a cadential figure containing a brief reminiscence of the earlier chromaticism in the second violin and viola (bars 36 and 38).

The 'development' takes up an inversion of the theme from bar 1, continuing with triadic extensions of the two-crotchet pattern that lead from the dominant region through E minor to a series of plagal cadences (G minor/ D) and a pedal D supporting further chromatic reminders before the recapitulation of the main theme at bar 63. From this point Mozart compresses much of the 'exposition' material: there is only one statement of the opening material, for instance (including an immediate reference to the countertheme in the cello at bar 68), and a shortened transition, continuing with the second subject in the tonic, G, at bar 74.

The Minuet is characterised by some delicate scoring that shows off the diverse colours of the quartet ensemble to fine effect. At the end of the first section the falling chromatic scale from D announced by the second violin is echoed by the viola in the same octave two bars later; at the end of the movement this phrase (now in the tonic, G) is subtly rescored for first violin and viola, an octave apart. A more telling illustration of colour contrast is Mozart's treatment of the first-violin melody of bars 28–36 which, when it returns in bars 81–9, is elegantly dovetailed between the three higher parts.

Mozart broadens the expressive range considerably in the minor-mode Trio. This also exhibits some sonata-like features, principally the clear separation of primary and secondary themes, the latter (bar 14ff.) being further developed at bar 39, after the tonic recapitulation of the main triadic material. In several respects this Trio is somewhat unsettling, in both phraseology and tonality. Although it begins symmetrically, bars 5–8 answering bars 1–4, the reprise of the unison opening phrase is extended in bars 12–13 by repetition of its concluding semitone rise (C sharp–D, D–E flat) lurching into a tonal no-man's-land. Instead of continuing in the expected dominant or relative-major key, Mozart starts out from the E flat pitch, left hanging in the air, as it were, and modulates into the relative major during the chorale-like dotted-minim chord sequence that follows, before swinging round at the last moment into the dominant, D. Neither is there the expected tonal continuity across the double-bar: the second section begins not with a reference to earlier material in the dominant, but with a new falling scale theme passing through, but not really settling upon, C minor and G minor (keys which are implied, rather than established) before the arrival of the preparatory chord of D major in bar 33. As in the Minuet, Mozart compresses his recapitulation, which is a modified repetition of bars 9–13, ending this time on the pitch C, from which the ensuing chorale chords weave their way back chromatically to the tonic, perhaps deliberately prefiguring the chromaticism of the imminent minuet da capo.

(3) Andante cantabile (C major)

The Andante cantabile is an abridged sonata form (a sonata form without a development section). Its main divisions are as follows: exposition: bars 1–51, incorporating secondary thematic material in the tonic from bar 7 (beginning in the cello and continuing in decorated form in the first violin); transitional material (from bar 14) modulating to the dominant region, G, via G minor (bar 25) and an extended dominant pedal on D supporting a sextuplet semiquaver pattern which migrates through the entire ensemble and leads into the second subject in the dominant (from bar 30^3), itself extended by several fleeting secondary ideas before the prolonged cadential paragraph, bars 43–8.

Four bars of punctuating chords in bars 48–51 shift the music back towards the tonic, C, after which the recapitulation largely retraces the steps of the exposition, but within the tonic. Mozart takes the opportunity to expand some of the exposition material, perhaps to compensate for the lack of a true 'development'. Reworking of earlier material within the recapitulation has been aptly termed 'secondary development' by Charles Rosen: 'The function of the secondary development is ... to reaffirm the tonic by moving to a subdominant area ... This secondary development, since it always modulates (however briefly) and touches upon subdominant keys, may use some of the material from the bridge [transition], or from a modulating passage of the exposition.'[6] By subdominant area, Rosen means keys on the flat side of the tonic, rather than just literally the subdominant key. In bars 58–69, for example, Mozart expands upon the transitional phrase originally heard at bar 7, introducing the new element of antiphony and then diverting the cello theme into darker harmonic territory (lingering in D flat at bars 63–5) and continuing by chromatic descent in the cello (supporting some diminished seventh and augmented sixth chords) towards the extended dominant pedal at bar 70. Further 'secondary development' is seen at bars 74–7 in which the first violin's demisemiquavers are accompanied by a sequentially founded quaver pattern in the second violin, derived from the material from bar 58, with the falling fifth here expanded to a seventh.

The Andante cantabile boasts a multiplicity of themes. Both of its main key-areas feature a wide range of contrasting ideas, many of them quite transitory in nature, for example at bars 4–6, 15–18, 30–4 and 34–8. Contrasting with these are themes elaborated in some detail, particularly within a contrapuntal (rather than melody–accompaniment) context – for example at bars 7–11, 25–30 and 42–8. For all this variety on the surface, however, the movement retains a satisfying coherence.

In part this has to do with the uniformly slow rate of harmonic change (frequently in dotted minim or minim–crotchet patterns), creating a basic consistency across the movement as a whole; and in part with Mozart's technique of thematic evolution which creates its own continuity. Consider, for instance, the progress of the three-quaver suffix that rounds off the opening thematic statement in bars 4–5. Initially, this figure has a descending stepwise melodic profile, modified in bar 5 to repetition of a single pitch; at bars 7–8 its function is altered, the repeated notes becoming a prefix to the imitative idea initiated by the cello; in bars 10–11 the violins continue the dialogue with yet another variant (three quavers followed by semiquavers); while in bars 15–16 a further development of the pattern acts as a countertheme to the semiquaver sextuplets beneath.

(4) Molto allegro

The finale is a combination of sonata form and fugue. It is not strictly fugal (unlike the finales of Haydn's quartets Op. 20 nos. 2 and 5, or Mozart's own earlier quartets K.168 and K.173) but instead incorporates fugato sections into its exposition and recapitulation. In this piece fugue becomes a means to an end, rather than an end in itself.

The movement opens with a fugal exposition (bars 1–17) equating to the first subject of a sonata-form exposition, setting out some of the main thematic material (a semibreve pattern and a lilting counter-theme) in the tonic key. At bars 51–91 a second fugato passage in the dominant key is equivalent to the sonata form's second subject. Its strongly syncopated character complements the 'neutral' semibreves of its predecessor, a factor highlighted when Mozart combines both fugue subjects from bar 69. Each fugato is followed by a contrasting episode in the idiom of a contredanse. That at bar 17 functions as a transitional passage, with learned counterpoint in 'bound style' from bar 31 and a subsidiary falling chromatic figure at bars 39–51 leading to an A major chord preparing the dominant key; the dance at bar 92 introduces additional thematic material within the dominant-key area, repeated straight away with variations to the articulation and accompaniment. Despite the stylistic opposition of fugue and dance, the position of each section within the scheme of a sonata exposition is clear enough. Everything is subsumed within the broad tonal plan of a modulation from tonic to dominant.

The opening fugato theme serves a vital role within the development section (bars 125–73); only the fugue theme, not a full fugal exposition, is used at this stage. After a passage extending a pithy chromatic tag, introduced right at the end of the exposition and swinging enharmonically to V/B flat minor at bars 141–2, the fugue theme is reconfigured in modulating antiphonal dialogue between the outer parts, in minor keys ascending by fifths, against a strongly articulated crotchet pattern in the middle of the texture that injects a greater sense of urgency into the proceedings. This continues to the end of the section, breaking off abruptly at bar 173 following an energetic chromatic (and canonic) descent.

The recapitulation begins with the contredanse tune from bar 17, but brought back in the subdominant, C (bar 175). The whole of the first-subject fugato is omitted. (Something akin to this procedure happens in the first movement of the D major Piano Sonata K.311, in which the recapitulation (bar 58) also begins in the subdominant with a subsidiary theme, the true first subject being delayed until the end of the movement.) In K.387 Mozart probably avoided a literal return to the opening fugal exposition at the start of the recapitulation because this would have entailed a serious loss of momentum, dissolving the texture back to a single polyphonic part in semibreves. The same textural 'gap' would have marred the restatement of the second subject by a literal tonic reprise of bar 51f.; so Mozart compresses the second subject fugato, recapitulating only the combined fugue themes from bar 69 at bar 209 (a strategy that retrospectively compensates for the omission of the first subject). The modified recapitulation (in which bars 175–209 are a literal transposition of bars 17–51) has the advantage of retaining the full texture and forward momentum at both these points.

Further development of the chromatic figure from bars 123–40 and a stretto presentation of the main theme follow in the coda (bars 268–98) whose last phrase brings this energetic movement to a surprisingly laid-back close.

K.421 in D minor

(1) Allegro moderato

Mozart's exposition is notable for the manner in which it places the first- and second-subject groups in stark opposition. Both groups are packed with rhythmic detail, often featuring small note-values very prominently, largely because of the relatively slow unit of pulse (four leisurely crotchet beats in a bar, rather than *alla breve*). The first group, whose opening theme is framed over a falling chaconne bass, D–C–B flat–A, makes only limited use of phrase repetition, the only significant example of which is at bar 5 (and even there the supporting harmonic progression is subtly altered). Thereafter, from bars 9 to 24, a succession of short and distinctive figures simply *evolves*, in a succession that Arnold Schoenberg characterised as 'prose-like in the unexcelled freedom of its rhythm and the perfect independence from formal symmetry'.[7]

Sharply contrasted with this is the second group which is wholly periodic in formation, presenting a series of regular, balanced phrases with wholesale, melodically decorated repetition, sometimes addition-

; variation of either texture (from bar 29) or register (bars
repetition of the second subject at bar 29 Mozart injects
polyphony of articulations, mixing together legato and
staccato attacks in just the right proportion to allow the soaring triplet
embellishments in the first violin to be heard clearly above the rest of
the ensemble.

Mozart treats us to a tightly organised development whose design
mirrors, to some extent, that of the exposition. It consists of two
'opposed' sections, the first (bars 42–58) returning to the 'prose' style
of the first-subject group and derived entirely from first-subject material, and the second (bars 59–69) countering once again with a more
periodic disposition. Mozart begins with a statement of bars 1 and 2 of
the main opening theme in the unusual key of E flat (the flat supertonic), supported again by the falling chaconne-like bass pattern; he
next makes novel use of the main theme's second bar (only) as a pedal
point in the viola and cello (bars 46–8), later introducing close stretto
imitation of bars 1 and 2 (to which a three-quaver countertheme is
added) and outlining an unusual succession of grating chromatic harmonies in two successive three-bar phrases (bars 53–8) that steadily
build up the tension to a point at which the resolution into G minor at
bar 59 initiates a welcome release. It is at this point that Mozart
returns to regular periodicity in a succession of one-bar phrases and a
uniform harmonic rhythm. The triadic semiquaver sextuplets that
formerly closed the exposition are put to new use as a countertheme to
the soaring new violin theme at bar 59ff. This marks out a circle-of-
fifths progression that moves ever closer to the tonic, D minor,
regained, via a reappearance of the triadic sextuplets in their original
cadential guise, at bar 70. All in all the development is an example of
Mozart's profound understanding of the potential of phrase-structure
to create 'form by contrast'. Bars 59–69 are a 'dynamic' resolution of
the 'stasis' of bars 42–58, a technique of form building that stands
outside all 'textbook' approaches of Mozart's time.

With the exception of a brief additional coda at bars 112b–17 highlighting upper and lower chromatic neighbour tones to the tonic note,
D, the recapitulation is straightforward (allowing for the displacement
of the second subject by half a bar at bar 94: compare bars 24–5),
adapting material to the tonic region as necessary.[8]

(2) Andante (F major)

Mozart's Andante is an episodic ternary structure: A (a + b, each part repeated) – B (a–b–a) – A (modified). While there is light imitation between the different instruments, the most important activity is in the first violin whose changing melodic profile defines the narrative. Its first section departs from the expected symmetrical phrase-lengths: while the section up to the first double-bar is eight bars long, it is divided unequally, the first articulating cadence falling on F in the middle of bar 5. Following the modulation to the dominant Mozart develops the opening theme through C minor and G minor, the new sequentially repeated suffix leading to repeated D major chords in bars 12 and 13. These take their rhythmic impetus from the idea first sounded at bars 2–3 and serve as a preparation for the return of the opening in the tonic, F. This reprise is diverted towards the subdominant (bars 20–2) before finally cadencing in the tonic once more with repetitions of the closing tag from bars 7–8.

The middle section turns to the tonic minor, introducing a rather more urgent three-quaver pattern (derived from bar 3) with staccato articulation, preceded by a prominent (legato) upbeat. It contrasts not only in mode and articulation, but in texture (note the transfer of leading melodic material to the cello at bars 30–4) and phraseology, moving entirely in balanced symmetrical periods, with the exception of the single-bar link (bar 51) back into a recapitulation of section A. The central episode subdivides into three paragraphs, of which the second, beginning in bar 35, is in A flat introducing running ornamental semiquavers in the first violin as a 'melodic' contrast to the surrounding 'motivic' material. The modified repeat of the A section is followed by a coda (bars 77–86) which once again returns to the rhythmic pattern of bars 2–3 to clinch the return to F at the end.

(3) Menuetto and Trio. Allegretto

As in the Andante, normal expectations of phraseology are confounded in the Minuet, whose first section is ten (not eight) bars long (an extension achieved by immediate sequential repetition of the pattern at bars 3–4). The sense of seamlessness in the phrasing results partly from the unobtrusive but telling rhythmic counterpoint between first violin and cello from bar 4: their falling melodic resolutions (a perfect fourth in the violin; a semitone in the cello) overlap, the cello's slurred dotted minim–crotchet always answering the violin a bar later. The cello's distinctive pattern is handed to the first violin near the start of the second section (over a pedal E), supported by sliding chromatics in the inner parts. A cadence in the dominant is interrupted at bar 22 by a quasi-development, founded on a modulating circle of fifths that is based on vigorous contrapuntal exchange of the initial dotted rhythm from bar 1, in which the ensemble is split into two antiphonal pairs of instruments (first violin/viola; second violin/cello), giving way to a literal recapitulation of the first ten-bar period.

This Minuet perfectly fits Charles Rosen's description of 'Minuet Sonata Form', a form

> in two parts but in three (large) phrases or periods: phrases two and three go together. In other words, the double bar is placed at the end of the first phrase, which may have a cadence either on the tonic or the dominant [here, in the tonic]. The second phrase either establishes or extends the dominant, develops it very briefly, and turns back to the tonic. The third phrase begins in the tonic and resolves or [as here] recapitulates ... the first period alone may be long enough both to define the tonic and to make a modulation, but not long enough to confirm the opposition of tonalities, or give this opposition sufficient solidity and mass to make it of any consequence. That task is therefore left to the second period ... [which] generally creates some of the polarity of tonic and dominant necessary to the late eighteenth-century composer, or it produces subsidiary modulations that increase the tension of the move away from the tonic.[9]

While harmonically unadventurous, the contrasting major-mode Trio (whose phrasing is entirely regular) is notable for its introduction of three effects: the 'scotch-snap' rhythm in the solo violin, the pizzicato accompaniment beneath and the unusual two-octave doubling of the theme when it is repeated on first violin and viola in bar 16. While almost embarrassingly lightweight on its own, the trio's naïvety makes a wonderful foil to the darker character of the Minuet.

(4) Variations: Allegretto ma non troppo

The theme is in binary form, featuring a siciliana rhythm to which a contrasting repeated-note pattern (bars 2–3, 10–11, 23–4) is opposed. As in many binary-form themes the opening of its second part makes a kind of 'rhyme' with the first, outlining the same siciliana rhythm, phrasing and texture. Mozart highlights this structural point in variations 1–3 by maintaining a corresponding 'rhyme' in terms of the prevailing figuration: in variation 1, for instance, bars 33–6 keep almost exactly to the same rhythms in both tune and accompaniment as bars 25–8.

Following normal eighteenth-century practice, Mozart applies a consistent figuration in each variation, featuring, successively, the first violin, second violin (producing cross-accents with the rest of the ensemble) and viola as soloists. Variation 2 presents a particularly intriguing texture of syncopations at two levels simultaneously (the second violin's part sounds like a diminution of the first's). From variation 3 Mozart departs from the theme's harmonic basis: at bar 69, for instance, the original Neapolitan E flat chord is replaced by diminished 7ths. In variations 4 (D major) and 5 (D minor, Più allegro) both phrasing and harmonic patterns are ruptured. In the former, the alteration of mode significantly affects the tonal structure in the second half (D – A replacing the original D minor – F) which is also curtailed by four bars. In the latter, the repeats are abandoned and the phraseology in the second half finally escapes that of the theme, all feeling of periodicity being suspended by the solo interjections of semiquaver triplets between bar 124 and bar 137. The recitative-like triplet semiquavers (derived from the repeated-note figures at bars 6–8 of the theme) suggest a heightened expressive purpose at the end.

K.458 in B flat

(1) Allegro vivace assai

This sonata-form movement, lasting 279 6/8 bars, is among the most extended in the 'Haydn' quartets. The significance of its 'chasse' topic (the initial 'hunting call' motif of bars 1–2) is dealt with in detail in Chapter 5.

Within the exposition each main and subsidiary thematic element is treated at length. Take, for example, the opening theme: this is an eight-bar phrase subdivided by an imperfect cadence on F at bar 4, and concluding with a firm tonic B flat (extended as a cello pedal). It is repeated in a new scoring beneath a trill in bar 26 and only at this point do we realise that the intervening passage, starting with the contrasting theme in thirds at bars 8–9 and featuring prominent soloistic semiquaver flourishes, was not in fact the start of a transition, but merely an intervening episode in a first subject that maps out a kind of ternary scheme. The real transition begins later at bar 27, returning to the semiquaver patterns and proceeding through some quaver syncopations to a weak imperfect cadence on C in bar 42.

Whether the motif that follows can be considered as a second subject is debatable. It outlines a dominant triad (F), but the stressed pitch is still C; moreover, the harmonic context, continuing at bar 47 with C–D flat alternations in the cello, suggests that this passage is really an extended 'secondary dominant' preparation for a stronger F major still to come. Bars 42–53 essentially prolong V/F, and are more memorable for their character of cadential closure (including rhyming cadences, bars 53/59) than for any specific secondary thematic function. Against these tonal manoeuvres, bar 54 sounds like a closing theme, although true 'closure' is withheld for some time yet. The ambiguity of thematic function within the second half of this exposition confirms the central importance of tonality, rather than theme, in defining classical sonata form. The identity of the true second subject is not the main issue here; what is most important is the transcending of the 'home' key by a new domain, in which Mozart can take the unusual step of indulging in some development of the second subject at bar 66, and a reprise of the 'episodic' theme of bars 8–9 sandwiched between a dominant pedal in the outer parts (bars 77–84) before the exposition is complete.

The development falls into three subsections: bars 91–106, introducing a new theme, which presents F major more strongly than any theme before the double-bar; 106–25, which develop a 'changing-note' figure, F–E–G–F–A flat, clearly related to that of bars 42–3 and 55, but with the semiquavers transferred on to the upbeat; and 126 to the end, an unmistakable reference to bars 42–3 is now set as a canon between the first violin and viola (bars 125–8) and subsequently viola and cello (bars 130–3, marking time over a dominant pedal). The 'changing-note' figure appears in a variety of contexts: as a solo (bars 106–14); and in antiphony between the three higher instruments (bars 114–16), adjacent pairs of instruments (bars 118–20) and the outer parts (bars 121–5), separating off main harmonic stages of the central development, from F minor (bar 106) through C minor and G minor to E flat (bar 126).

Within the recapitulation (bars 137–230) Mozart retains the outline of the exposition with occasional departures, such as the subdominant digression at bars 168ff., securing the arrival of the first of the ambiguous second-subject motifs in the tonic region at bar 182.

In the sizable coda (lasting slightly longer than the development section) Mozart treats the main 'hunting' theme (ignored in the 'true' development section) to an astonishing variety of stretto presentations within a short period of time, saturating the whole ensemble (bars 238–52). The sheer density of counterpoint here creates an accumulation of activity which turns this coda into the climax of the whole movement, superseding the normal function of the recapitulation. There is another reference to bars 42–3 (including yet more stretto at bar 262) before Mozart closes with a brief nod at the 'changing-note' figure from bar 106ff., this time as a cadential close – a final reminder of the flexibility of thematic function within this sonata structure.

(2) Menuetto and Trio. Moderato

The Minuet's first section is an eight-bar phrase divided unequally, 3 + 5 bars, and ending in the tonic, B flat. Its obvious imbalance is stressed still further by the strong accents on the third beat of bars 3, 4 and 5. Phrase irregularity continues after the double-bar: two sequential two-bar units (the second melodically decorated), followed by a three-bar cadential progression into a five-bar inverted pedal F, falling at bar 21 into a reprise of the lopsided eight-bar opening. One has the distinct impression that this movement was harmonically, rather than melodically, inspired; virtually all of its thematic material simply fastens on to preconceived cadential formulae.

The Trio reveals rather finer melodic distinction, particularly in its second section which contains some telling chromaticism at bars 13–14 and 22–4. After the reprise of the opening theme (bar 19) Mozart incorporates developments of some of the features of bars 5–10, for example the octave leap (bar 7) expanded to an octave-plus-seventh and imitated between the first violin and cello at bars 25–6.

(3) Adagio (E flat major)

This intense Adagio, in abridged sonata form, incorporates a wide range of expression, providing a serious counterweight to the sunny, jocular character of the other movements of K.458. Although Mozart did not specify 'affetuoso' in his tempo heading, melodies such as that for the first violin at bars 7–11 or that for the cello in bar 18, against a throbbing chordal accompaniment, clearly call for that quality in their execution. Every bar is governed by precise dynamic or articulation marks which require careful attention from the players. The opening theme, for instance, depends as much upon the contrasts of *piano* and *sforzando*, legato and staccato for its effect as upon the actual pitches.

Concealed beneath the hyper-refined melodic façade, lies a straightforward harmonic skeleton. Bars 7–14, for example, form the 'transition' between the first and second subjects of the exposition: the first four bars move in sequential stages from C minor through B flat major–minor towards the secondary dominant F, though its arrival is obscured both by the abrupt register transfer from first violin to cello half-way through the bar, and by the chromatic part-writing, eventually coalescing to form an augmented-sixth chord on the second beat of bar 11 (*forte*), whose resolution (*piano*) to the target pitch, F, goes almost unnoticed. The dominant key, B flat, follows in the middle of bar 14.

The second subject (bars 15–24) subdivides into three portions: bars 15–18, 16–21 and 21–4 (regaining the tonic, E flat, once again at the end, leading straight into the recapitulation). By itself, Mozart's sequentially designed theme is not particularly distinguished, but gains in wistfulness by its integration with the sliding chromatic progression beneath, to which it perhaps arose as a kind of 'descant' (frustratingly, the autograph discloses no clues as to its precise origin). Bars 16–21 are a textural inversion of the previous phrase, with the theme transferred from first violin to cello, while bars 21–4 are cadentially conceived.

Unusually for these quartets, the recapitulation radically transforms the order of the exposition materials. Bars 3–5 of the exposition are omitted in the reprise, which continues instead with reworkings of the rising E flat arpeggio deflecting the tonality towards F minor for the modified transition at bar 29. The motif of bars 3–5 is reserved instead for the end of the movement (bars 47–50) where it precedes a further appearance of the arpeggio figure of bars 2–3. Evidently Mozart foresaw that an unchanged repetition of the end of the second-subject group, with its intense rhythmic activity, would not prove a suitable ending to the movement, and noticed that the falling chromatic line of bars 3–5 would make a suitable 'closing' gesture (especially when repeated after the interrupted cadence on C minor in bar 48), dissipating the tension and leading into a final appearance of the E flat arpeggio of bars 2–3 and concluding *pianissimo* gesture.

The polythematic surface of K.458's Adagio masks some sophisticated phraseology. Since the pace is so slow, it is appropriate to count in crotchet beats rather than bars. In addition to the restatement of the opening theme in bars 5–6 (which features a half-bar displacement) and any sequential repetitions, there are at least six distinct ideas within these fourteen bars, of which three are encountered in the first four bars. If one allows for the subdivision of the theme beginning in bar 7 into three discrete components, each with its own characteristic rhythmic or accentual profile, the number of ideas multiplies still further. Indeed, in rhythmic terms alone, this opening section is amazingly diverse, encompassing even sextuplet semiquavers in bars 9 and 10. Mozart's phraseology is remarkably sophisticated, resolving even and odd numbers of beats within a broader symmetry. In the first five bars there are three successively longer thematic elements (four, six and eight crotchet beats respectively), giving the impression of continuous 'growth' throughout, while the second subject's antecedent phrase (bars 14^3–17^2) incorporates an element of 'foreshortening' that might be represented as follows:

2 beats (introduction: 14^{3-4})

   4 beats (15^{1-4})

      3 beats (16^{1-3})

         3 (= 1 + 1 + 1) beats (16^4, 17^1, 17^2)

Alternatively, the entire phrase might be felt as 6 + 6 beats (bars 14^3–15^4, 16^1–17^2), counting the two beats of throbbing semiquaver preparation for the first-violin theme. In this case, there is an intriguing ambiguity – probably deliberate – concerning the relationship of bars 15^{1-3} and 16^{1-3} which sound as if rhymed, but actually fall at different points within their successive phrases. Such an effortless technique of asymmetrical phrase building and subdivision (in which rests seem to play as important a part as notes) is one of the hallmarks of Mozart's compositional maturity.

(4) Allegro assai

The finale, in sonata form, is a triumph of organisation.

Its main outlines are as follows:

Exposition (bars 1–133) including a long transition to the C major harmony (bars 16–46) which prepares for the second subject in F at bar 48 (followed by a huge variety of contrasting material at bars 64ff., 82ff. (a genuine 'third' subject, arguably more of a contrast to the main theme than bar 48's triplets), 97ff. (compare bar 16), 113 ('brilliant style' cadential material) and 122 (an F major reminder of the first theme));

Development (bars 134–97) based exclusively on the first subject, and subdivided at bar 165, thereafter returning by degrees to the tonic, B flat, for the reprise of the main theme in bar 199;

A regular recapitulation preserving all the main exposition features in order, and ending decisively on the tonic, B flat, with a slight extension of the exposition's closing material.

One of the most striking features of this movement is the prominence of octave writing, especially between the two violins. This device (bars 9–16 and 22–34, for instance), produces a texture reminiscent of Mozart's 1772 Divertimentos, K.136–8 (the finale of K.136, for instance), and the 1774 Serenade, K.203 (especially its Prestissimo finale). At times Mozart appears to break out beyond the normal dimensions of a quartet into quasi-orchestral textures (bars 113–21 and 307–13).

Mozart combines in this movement all the hallmarks of the mature classical style (periodic phrasing, precisely articulated melody, dynamic contrast, flexibility of texture, tonal drama and so forth) with the rigour of baroque counterpoint, achieving that ideal blend of 'horizontal' and 'vertical' dimensions that is so conspicuously lacking in the 'galant' quartets K.155–60 and K.168–73. Whereas those quartets are satisfying either as elegant galant melody and accompaniment or as quasi-baroque fugues, the finale of K.458 achieves a masterly integration of both idioms. The texture is kaleidoscopic in its variety but is at the same time carefully regulated by a network of textural and thematic cross-references drawing upon the resources of counterpoint, all in the service of a dramatically unfolding form.

The relationship between the 'first' and 'second' subjects provides a good illustration of textural cross-referencing. Thematically, the two are quite distinct, but the latter (bars 48–56) retains something of the former's profile since it too depends on solo–ensemble contrast: whereas bars 1–8 unfold as a series of two-bar 'solo'–'ensemble' alternations, bars 48–56 reverse the process, with the ensemble taking the leading role and the solo violin providing links between successive statements.

Examples of thematic cross-referencing within the exposition include: (i) the continuation beyond the opening statement of the main theme (bars 1–16) which takes up the concluding suffix (bars 15–16) of that theme in the two lower instruments in antiphony with the violins; (ii) the richly scored contrapuntal passage beginning at bar 97 (a subsidiary element of the second-subject group) which refers back once again to the motif of bars 15–16 and which is restated immediately in invertible counterpoint (bar 106ff., where the motif is transferred from cello to second violin); and (iii) the concluding exposition material, which is a version of the main opening theme at bar 122.

In the development section imitative counterpoint comes decisively to the fore. At bar 140 there is a brief stretto presentation of the main theme, continuing with three further sequential statements by the first violin, giving rise to a succession of paired entries descending through the texture (bars 149–61) and including a powerful descending suspension chain leading ultimately to a cadence on D (V/G minor) which marks the end of the first stage of the development. The second stage, which takes place largely in the context of extended pedal points, introduces entries of the main theme in partial augmentation (bar 169) and in closely packed stretto (bar 183ff.), and includes some antiphonal fragmentation of bar 2 of the theme (bars 179–81). In retrospect, the introduction of the dense contrapuntal passage in invertible counterpoint at bar 97 of the exposition can be seen as foreshadowing this action-packed development, another example of Mozart's use of contrapuntal procedures as a form-building device.

K.428 in E flat

(1) Allegro non troppo

Mozart's hushed unison opening, notable for its angular, chromatic movement, appears strangely peripheral to the remainder of the exposition material. James Baker has pointed out that it announces nine of the twelve possible chromatic pitches and that, following a diatonic four-bar answering phrase, the opening returns in a richly harmonised restatement *forte* at bar 12, in which the 'missing' three pitches are supplied, thus justifying the restatement as an 'aggregation' of all twelve tones.[10] The cello's rhythm underlying this rich chordal passage has a kind of built-in 'accelerando' from bar 13, spanning successively shorter units of seven beats, three beats and finally two beats, the dotted quaver–semiquavers toppling hell-bent into the long transition which follows. This is characterised by continual melodic evolution, in which, accompanied by a leisurely pace of chord change, the fluid first-violin melody of bars 16–17 gradually crystallises into falling scale-snippets at bars 20–1, later infiltrating the whole texture from bar 24: it is adapted to serve as a bass line beneath punctuating quaver chords (bars 29–30); acquires a new countertheme (bars 31–3); and finally prepares the chordal build-up to a massive cadence with 6/4 trill, closing in B flat major in bars 34–6.[11]

The tonal status of the second subject beginning in bar 40 is somewhat clouded, circumnavigating the dominant, B flat, by introducing its related degrees of G minor, F major and C minor, rather than stating it directly (a second perfect cadence in the new key only arrives at bars 47–8). Rescored for viola with an imitative continuation for just the two lower parts, it gives way to the exposition's closing material. The falling scale pattern, like the transition but in uniform minims and interrupted by a *forte* cadence after three bars, is stated first in the major, then in the minor mode leading to a strongly defined chromatic cadence (bars 62–4) and closing semiquaver flurries.

Although there is no obvious thematic connection between the peculiar opening phrase and the rest of the exposition, one consistent feature which assists its coherence is the element of *piano* and *forte* dynamic contrast. It is present at every stage: for example the restatement of the theme at bar 12; the falling quaver steps at bar 24; the injection of the countertheme in bar 31; the second-subject theme itself (bar 40, bar 42); the cadential interruption of the closing passage (bar 58); even the articulating cadence at bars 63–4, before the peroration.

This element of dynamic contrast continues into the freely constructed development, highlighting its alternation between virtuosic triplet arpeggios passed throughout the texture and the pithy grace-note figure introduced in bar 75, following the imitative presentation of the main theme (the only exposition material used).[12] Allowing for occasional rescorings of exposition material (the second violin replaces the viola at bar 144, for instance) the recapitulation proceeds exactly according to plan, excepting only a brief extension of the second violin's interjection at bar 108.

(2) Andante con moto

The Andante con moto is a full-scale sonata form. Its first subject (bars 1–10) features a triadic bass over which Mozart weaves a tenuous melody comprising a rising 4th and syncopated scale descent. The irregular five-bar phrase with which Mozart opens is a good illustration of Riepel's principle of phrase extension by means of internal repetition.[13] By continuing the theme and its bass from the end of bar 3 straight into bar 5 we would arrive at the 'normal' outline; Mozart's bar 4 is an internal sequential repetition of bar 3. Riepel's view was that such local irregularities were best 'smoothed out' by repetition, resulting in a larger symmetry (5 + 5 bars, and so on). In this case, Mozart exactly follows Riepel's prescription, for he continues with a balancing five-bar phrase, producing an overall symmetrical ten-bar period, the first phrase (*Einschnitt*) ending on the tonic degree (*Grundabsatz*), the second with an imperfect cadence on the dominant (*Quintabsatz*).

The rest of the exposition illustrates one of the problems of applying nineteenth-century formal models to eighteenth-century sonata forms. Beginning at the upbeat quaver to bar 11 is *either* a second subject (bars 10^6–14^5 are more melodic than anything else before the double-bar) – in which case there is no separate transition (the imperfect cadence *on* E flat in bar 10 being followed abruptly by the secondary theme *in* the dominant) – *or* it is a long transition section – in which case there is no clearly defined second subject. Nineteenth-century sonata form prescriptions require both elements. Either of the two schemes would be satisfying within eighteenth-century understandings of the form, since bars 1–35 outline the expected contrast of tonic and dominant keys, the keys being more fundamental than their thematic expression (which is not especially strong at any point). Possibly the first of the above alternatives is more plausible, since the function of a normal transition is to modulate towards the related key (or even its dominant) and bars 10^6–35 seem remarkably stable for all their melodic and harmonic chromatic inflections, and even feature subsidiary dominant-key material in bars 23–4 subsequently resolved within the now firmly established key of E flat. Whatever the precise structural interpretation, the withholding of closure until bar 35 is quite remarkable.

The development (bars 36–55) is derived entirely from the first subject and its supporting triadic patterns. Here Mozart takes delight in the sheer variety of harmony and textures possible with his triadic figure. He indulges in invertible counterpoint throughout, treating either the syncopated line or the arpeggiated bass quavers as treble or bass, and introducing intervallic inversion at bar 46 (falling 5th in the cello – augmented – replacing the rising 5th of bar 36, itself derived from the restatement of the opening theme at bar 7) and bar 47 (falling quaver triad). In the recapitulation Mozart continues to develop second-subject figures (now within the tonic region) at bars 66–78.

An important feature of the movement as a whole is the element of thematic transformation, which assures coherence beneath the surface diversity. The idea first stated by the first violin in bars 10^4–11 undergoes two types of transformation, intervallic and textural. At bar 15ff. its anacrusic falling sixth, G–B flat, becomes instead a rising chromatic semitone echoing between viola and first violin. At this point the texture also changes, from treble theme and homophonic three-part accompaniment to interlocking pairs of instruments. This process of evolution is carried still further at bar 19, where the pairing changes (first violin/cello, second violin/viola) along with intervallic inversion in the outer parts. These successive stages in the evolution of the second subject are linked by strong rhythmic identity: one never loses sight of the starting-point for the whole of bars 10^6–22, which emerge almost as a single thought.

(3) Menuetto and Trio. Allegro.

The Minuet is a miniature sonata form whose first subject comprises two elements, the upbeat leaping figure and the slurred quaver pairs, leading on repetition to the second subject in B flat (bars 11–12) followed by a subsidiary figure over a held chord and closing pattern (bars 22–6). This is separated from the 'recapitulation' by a contrasting episode (in the tonic, E flat), rather than a development, introducing a new motif and prefiguring the first subject at its end (second violin, bars 34–5), making the actual reprise in the first violin sound like an echo. The second subject is brought back within the tonic at bar 48, and the original subsidiary idea is expanded into a magnificently full-textured *fortissimo* replete with canonic cross-accents just before the close.

By contrast the Trio, in B flat, is more developmental. Its first section closes with a reference to a portion of the opening theme (bars

10–11) which is put to imitative use in the second section, appearing at bars 22–5 in a dialogue between viola and first violin, in the cello at bars 26–7 and finally at the top of the texture at the close. Tonally, the trio is unusual: its first half begins in C minor (the relative minor of the Minuet) and modulates conclusively into B flat only in its last four bars, while its second section begins in G minor and moves on to F (preceded by a neat viola pick-up) from bars 22–9, forming a long preparation for B flat, in which key it ends (followed, of course by a da capo reprise of the E flat Minuet).

(4) Allegro vivace

The initially light-hearted finale of K.428 conceals moments of high drama, revealed later on. Though its character is that of a rondo, it is actually a sonata form whose first-subject group (bars 1–34) is a binary structure featuring a subdivided 'A' section (bars 1–8, 9–16). Its opening is characterised by slurred quaver pairs marking out a distinctive scansion with the main weight in the second half of the phrase; after the central double-bar the slurred pattern is treated to antiphony, returning, after some Haydnesque trickery with the accents and phrasing, to its original shape (bar 27) now elided with the semiquaver passage from bar 9. The ensuing transition (bar 35ff.) begins with a chordal quaver figure featuring *forte–piano* contrast and continuing with a striding arpeggio figure imitated between the violins that stresses the submediant, C minor, in preparation for a modulation to the dominant, B flat (preceded by its own dominant, F, in bars 58–9). The second subject (bar 60) is repeated in varied scoring at bar 76, including a triplet accompaniment passed between the two lower parts, before dissolving into surging semiquaver roulades at bar 90 over repeated tonic–dominant cadential progressions (and exploiting the contrasted pairings of first and second violins, and second violin/ viola). A subsidiary theme follows (bars 110–18, repeated at bars 118– 26), closing with a pattern of descending interlocking thirds (first violin, bar 117, bar 125) that is separated at bar 127, and from bar 131 is inverted with a two-note quaver suffix (bar 132) that is finally fragmented and played off between the higher and lower instruments preparing rhythmically for the return of the first subject at bar 140.

There follows an exact recapitulation of the opening period (but without repeats) leading to a tonally modified transition beginning at bar 174. Subdominant colouring is suggested at first, proceeding in the direction of F minor before an abrupt sideways shift heralds a G minor entry of the striding arpeggio figure at bar 186, this time treated to a full-scale sequential repetition and additional contrapuntal entries in the viola, turning through F minor and B flat before attaining E flat at bar 207. The remainder of the 'retransition' and second subject unfold as before. A substantial coda (bars 297–342) is appended, adapting the main theme to some new contexts. It sounds against a soaring countertheme in the first violin in bars 305–12, and at bar 321 is transferred (in thirds) to the middle of the texture between tonic pedals in the outer parts, eventually dissolving in antiphonal exchanges (bars 329–34). The finale ends dramatically with four bars of whispered *pianissimo* answered by the four triumphant cadential chords.

K.464 in A

(1) Allegro

Two features dominate this movement: it makes almost obsessive use of the rhythm of the first bar of the opening theme (though it is far from being 'monothematic'), and it is strongly characterised by the kind of regular, symmetrical phrasing that typifies the classical style. Its opening paragraph, for instance, begins with two four-bar phrases moving harmonically from tonic to dominant and back again. At bar 8 the initial rhythm is fragmented and repeated sequentially, but this pattern and its answering phrase still fall within a balanced framework leading to a strong tonic close in bar 16. Even adapted to an imitative contrapuntal context (bars 17–24) the main opening still marks off regular four-bar periods. Only within the second-subject group does this regularity begin to break down: the second subject, itself a perfectly balanced 'downbeat' phrase (bars 37–44), is treated to stretto imitation upon its restatement at bar 45, and in the course of the rising harmonic sequence is extended to five bars (49–53). Otherwise, the second-subject group is also quite symmetrical, continuing with syncopated canonic flurries in the middle of the ensemble and including just one prominent irregular pattern (bars 62–8) amid a succession of four- and two-bar melodic units. Unusually, Mozart returns to the first subject at the end of the exposition (bars 69–87), adapted to cadential contexts.

The development, which is the most extended in this set of quartets (lasting 74 bars, over one-third of the length of the entire movement), focuses almost entirely on the main opening theme. Beginning in the dominant minor, it first introduces the theme in imitation at two bars' distance. Next, Mozart treats it as a cadential close, like the end of the exposition (bars 96–9). Following this is (i) a kind of 'rhythmic stretto' based on the dotted crotchet and three-quaver pattern (bars 99–103); (ii) a succession of paired dialogue entries of the main theme with its upbeat restored and leading from the G major 7th chord at bar 105 to one on C sharp (V/F sharp) at bar 122; and (iii) a passage based on just the rhythmic pattern, at first in triadic guise accompanied by crotchet chord punctuations beneath, and later incorporating some antiphony between the first violin and the lower instruments, gradually stretching across the whole texture (bars 123–42) and coalescing in paired dialogue and close stretto at bar 143. Even the cello's pedal E, heralding the recapitulation, supports yet another transformation of the main theme in the violins (bars 150–8).

The recapitulation, perhaps surprisingly, retains all of the exposition material, including the striking 'transition' passage, which instead of modulating into the dominant (or dominant of the dominant) audaciously introduces a memorable tune in a key one semitone higher than the eventual destination (C major, preparing the dominant of the dominant, B, in the exposition; F, preparing the dominant, E, in the recapitulation). One might think that, in a movement in which the main idea had been so comprehensively discussed, some compression of that idea would be allowed in the recapitulation (as is the case in, for example, the finale of K.387). But Mozart does not sacrifice a single bar; in fact, the closing exposition material is expanded somewhat, incorporating additional treatment of bar 2 of the main theme (bars 242–9) and an energetic final four-bar peroration, *forte*, with the theme in octaves.

(2) Menuetto and Trio

This is one of the most closely organised of Mozart's minuets, being built almost exclusively around three motifs: (i) the unison opening; (ii) the first violin's four-bar continuation; and (iii) the rising stepwise fourth in the second violin, bars 5–8. All three interact in a number of different permutations in the course of the piece – for instance, (ii) and (iii) at bars 5–8; (i) and (ii) at bars 9–12 – while imitation is rife: (i) in stretto imitation with itself at bar 13ff., (ii) likewise at bar 17ff. etc. The second half, which is as developmental as many a sonata-form development section, introduces inversions of texture (bars 29–32 are recast in bars 34–7) and of motifs (i) and (ii), as at bars 38–41, which features motif (ii) in inversion against itself; and bars 57–8 which perform a similar operation on motif (i). This last occurs after the recapitulation of the opening (bar 55), as does the complex combination of strands at bars 59–62 where, in addition to theme–countertheme pairing of (i) and (ii), Mozart places (ii) in stretto with itself. Arnold Schoenberg was fond of this Minuet as a teaching device, praising its 'development of a motive by variation' and its contrapuntal treatment which 'does not vary the motive, but displays the possibilities of combination inherent in the basic theme or themes'.[14]

The Trio, in E, is in complete contrast to this close motivic working. Its richer texture (melody and accompaniment throughout) features an episode of energetic triplet arpeggios after the double-bar (exploring the dominant region) before returning to the opening phrase at bar 25, in which both melody and accompaniment are embellished.

3. Andante

For the Andante of K.464 Mozart chose a variation structure. Its plan (examined further from the rhetorical point of view in Chapter 5) is quite straightforward, one of countless examples of 'harmonic' variation in which successive statements progressively embellish the binary-form theme (8 + 10 bars, each repeated, with a modulation to the dominant at the mid-point over an unchanging harmonic foundation).

Variation 1 introduces melodic decorations in the first violin, in continuous demisemiquavers, whose function changes in variation 2, where they are transferred into the middle of the texture as a kind of ostinato. In variation 3 the texture shifts significantly, highlighting a dialogue between the upper and lower pairs of instruments before all four combine in the final cadential approach. Dialogue is explored further in the following, *minore*, variation, which additionally offers a new rhythmic aspect (triplet semiquavers) to help define a shift in scoring across the double-bar (first violin/cello, giving way to second violin/viola). In variation 4 the second part is extended to fourteen bars. The intensely imitative variation 5, fully written out and curtailing the second part to eight bars, without repeat-marks, extends the dialogue idea still further, hinting at canon 4 × 2 between the upper and lower pairs of instruments at the opening and engaging in more rapid shifts of texture than previously attempted. For instance, at bar 102 (the written-out repeat of the opening bars) the canonic pairing is retained, but the instrumental grouping shifts to first violin/viola, second violin/cello. At bar 110 the inner two instruments are paired; at bar 118ff., which form a climax to this variation, Mozart introduces four-in-one imitation of the dotted figure within which the pairings shift still more rapidly (virtually every two bars, up to the final cadence).

There is good reason to think of the three central variations as a 'sub group' whose larger purpose is a demonstration of the possibilities of dialogue within the quartet idiom. Each possesses strikingly individual characteristics and yet plays its part in defining the broader formal picture of this movement. Variation 6 returns to the original 8 + 10 phraseology (with repeats). It focuses on the ostinato concept of variation 2, though with a more distinctive rhythmic element in the cello ticking away beneath the serene, almost chorale-like, legato lines of the first violin, second violin and viola. The extended coda which follows (bars 144–86) makes further use of this rhythmic figure, which migrates gradually upwards through the texture before dissolving into a restatement of the opening in something approaching its original texture and harmonisation (though comprising the original bars 1–4 followed by bars 12–18), and ending with reminders of variation 5 (bars 174–7) and the cello ostinato of variation 6.

As in the finale of K.421, Mozart attempts, in variations 1–4 of K.464, to create musical 'rhymes' by repeating more or less exactly the rhythm or texture of the opening immediately after the double-bar. For instance, in variation 1 the exact rhythmic pattern of the first violin's demisemiquavers along with its supporting accompaniment in bars 18–19 recurs at bars 26–7, and in variation 3 the pairing of instruments (violins *versus* viola/cello) is retained at bars 62–4. As the variations proceed Mozart departs more and more from the original harmonic scheme, as, for instance, at bars 60–1 and 69–72 (variation 3) and more radically in variation 4, the second part of which extends a dominant pedal A through its first half. In variation 5 almost all traces of the original harmonic pattern are lost.

(4) Allegro non troppo

This sonata-form movement is infused with counterpoint. Beginning with a falling chromatic theme and countertheme pairing, its first-subject group continues with contrapuntal textures of various kinds: paired instruments in dialogue (bars 8–14), a restatement of the opening material with imitation at one bar's distance (bar 17), close stretto (bars 29–32) answered by the violins (bars 31–8). The second group is dominated by pedal points: Mozart redeploys the opening chromatic theme imitatively over a pedal E, which is then transferred into the middle of the texture against the original countertheme now in tenths (bar 50). The closing cadential portion of this exposition (bars 66–81) is also largely over a pedal, a feature that spills into the development, the pedal G following an abrupt modulation to the dominant of B minor. Much of the development treats the chromatic theme alongside a new countertheme (violins, bars 95–6) and in the context of a long-range circle-of-fifths harmonic progression extending from G major through A minor (bars 96–7), B minor (98–9), C sharp major (100–101) and returning at double the harmonic speed through F sharp, B, E and A before cadencing on a chord of C sharp (bar 113). A second abrupt break in continuity occurs here with the introduction of a chorale-like *alla breve* section in mock species counterpoint, note-against-note, later decorated with continuous quavers in the second violin.

Following an almost regular recapitulation (Mozart repeats the first-violin roulade in bars 203–4 once again in bars 209–10, and alters some of the precise disposition of the counterpoint) the movement closes with an extended coda that takes up the development's new repeated-quaver countertheme (specifically the first-violin component from bar 96) in invertible counterpoint against the main theme's chromatic element. At bar 233, for instance, the chromatic theme is in the treble with the quaver countertheme beneath; in bar 236, the situation is reversed. Bars 236–48 continue in the same vein, with theme and countertheme migrating throughout the texture while incorporating some thematic 'fragmentation' of the main theme for good measure (the legato lines at bars 242 and 245 are constructed from sequences of just its first four chromatic notes). The finale ends *pianissimo*, casually converting the opening chromatic theme into a closing cadential one.

K.465 in C

(1) Adagio. Allegro

The Adagio introduction to K.465 is the source of the quartet's nickname, the 'Dissonance'. Actually, it contains only mild vertical dissonances, such as the brief whole-tone clusters at the beginning of bars 3 and 7; otherwise the chords in themselves (founded on a chromatically descending bass line that is not at all unusual in the classic period)[15] are unproblematic to describe within eighteenth-century tonality.[16] What is unusual is the particular shifting succession of chords in bars 1–9, blurring our perspective as it unfolds, and the fact that these bars, considered from the tonal point of view, do not establish C at all clearly from the outset. In bar 1 the repeated cello Cs may at first suggest a tonic (though ambiguously, in the absence of chordal references); however, once the other strands of polyphony begin to enter in bars 1–4 Mozart seems instead to be setting up a first-inversion chord of A flat, but then veers off towards a chromatically enhanced G in bars 3–4. This much – a hint of C followed by several beats' worth of G – suggests that C is indeed the tonic until bar 5, which starts a sequential repetition of the preceding phrase one whole tone lower. For all the chromaticism which follows, bars 9–16 do begin to outline C as the most plausible 'pole of attraction', although the picture clarifies only slowly and retrospectively as we begin to link together such tell-tale signs as the harmonic falling steps in bars 9–12, each outlining just one implied chord per bar, the progression from bar 13 (fundamentally a dominant-seventh chord on G) to the first beat of bar 14 (C major) and the resolution of the augmented-sixth chord, A flat–C(–D)–F sharp, on to G major in bars 15–16. A dominant preparation ensues, pitting the cello against the rest of the ensemble and coming to rest on an unambiguous dominant-seventh chord in bar 22. The suspense created throughout this section is successfully achieved by the withholding of clear tonal (and for a while, accentual) reference points: a blurred image adjusted into sharp focus.

The ensuing Allegro, in a crystal clear C major, comes as a welcome relief. Its innocuous eight-bar opening phrase consists of a sequentially repeated two-bar unit answered by a four-bar melody generated largely out of repetitions of a prominent falling sixth. In effect, this phrase is a kind of miniature 'development', built out of its first two bars. Bars 25 and 26 are a sequence of the whole of bars 23 and 24; bar 27 begins as a further sequence of bar 23; and bars 28 and 29 are constructed out of progressively shorter fragments of the preceding material. While it is possible theoretically to reconcile this advanced phrase construction with the prescriptions of Joseph Riepel referred to earlier in this chapter (it may be said to incorporate 'internal repetitions' of a figure from the middle of the phrase), such sophistication merely serves to highlight the gulf that existed between theory and the best classical practice.

Mozart's opening phrase is then repeated with the addition of snatches of terse counterpoint in the viola and cello, continuing with a hint of the subdominant and a touch of syncopation before settling at bar 44 into stretto entries of the main theme in a transition section reaching D major at bar 55. *En route* is another instance of thematic 'development'. The first violin's semiquavers in bar 50 generate a dialogue in the following two bars, now on alternate beats – a rhythmic 'gear-change' that gives rise also to the ascending scales in bars 53 and

54. Similarly 'developmental' is the treatment of the longer pattern of semiquavers in bar 57. Originally a 'suffix', following the striking scale descent of bar 56, this changing-note pattern turns into a 'prefix' in bar 59, echoing between first violin and viola, and bar 61, where it serves as a bass to a soaring treble theme before the texture once again fragments.

The second-subject group (beginning at bar 56 in G major) is subdivided by the cadence at bar 71, after which a subsidiary theme enters, introducing triplet values and later syncopated off-beat entries (bars 77–83). Having reached a second articulating G major cadence at bar 91, Mozart closes the exposition with a reminder of the opening main theme (subsequently inverted at bar 96) in the course of which the theme appears as a perfectly good bass line (bar 99), preparing for the return to C major.

The development is entirely derived from this main theme. Beginning with a subdominant implication over a pedal B flat, with imitation of the theme at two bars' distance, the music heads in the direction of D minor (implied by bars 111–14, which outline a dominant-seventh chord on A), but swings at bar 115 to a dominant seventh (on F) whose expected resolution (on to B flat) is once again thwarted: it is treated instead as an augmented-sixth chord – F–A–C–D sharp – resolving on to E (V/A minor) at bar 121. From this point the theme acts as a bass against an urgent new quaver motif before dissolving into a staccato pattern based on the rhythm of the main theme without its initial minim tie. This figure, in imitation between the outer parts with strongly syncopated in-filling from the second violin and viola, is the climactic section of the development – indeed, perhaps of the whole movement – touching on A minor, D minor, G minor and C minor (bars 125–39) before a second series of falling sequential steps (bars 139–42) leads eventually (bar 147) to a further appearance of the texture from bar 121ff. This heralds the return of the opening at bar 155, marked by a hint of the subdominant at bar 156 and a contrapuntal reworking of the counterstatement beginning at bar 163. The end of the recapitulation (like that of the exposition) does not cadence but leads chromatically into the repeat and subsequently the coda.

The coda (bars 227–46) begins with a harmonic reminiscence of the start of the development (implied subdominant and supertonic), continuing with further contrapuntal imitations of the main theme supporting a prominent new cadential theme in *opera buffa* style at the top of the texture (bars 235–8) and new derivations from its rhythm (as at bars 235–6 and 238–9), before closing quietly over a tonic pedal.

(2) *Andante cantabile*

This movement, another abridged sonata form, is the expressive 'heart' of the quartet. The first-subject group, bars 1–25, incorporates a statement of the main theme (bars 1–4, answered by bars 5–8 and confirmed by the further four-bar cadential theme, bars 9–12); and a transitional passage features a motif made from an 'échappée' pattern (C–B natural–D–C in the first violin, bar 13) and announced in dialogue between the outer parts with chordal in-filling from the second violin and viola (bars 13–25).

The second-subject group, bars 26–44, starts out from the dominant degree, C, and is based on imitations of a repeated-note figure and suspensions. The imitations then unfold over a decorated ostinato in semiquavers in the cello. It concludes with two strong cadential chords (bars 26–31), and with a passage that recasts the repeated-note figure chordally before closing on an elided C major cadence (bar 39). Here the 'transition' motif enters again (its echoes accelerated this time, at bars 41–3) leading back to a decorated tonic recapitulation (bar 45).

The decorated recapitulation includes the expected tonal modifications (and a superb enrichment of the original transition, bars 58–74). It follows the outline of the exposition until bar 85; a 'secondary development' introduces a repeat of bars 75–8 with minor-key inflections and an extension through F minor, leading by a circle of fifths through A flat and back, and culminating in a richly scored and chromatically enhanced reprise of the chordal pattern of bars 81–4, closing into the tonic major at bar 101.

In the coda Mozart returns to the 'transitional' motif, placing it now in the second violin against a throbbing semiquaver accompaniment and a contrasting countertheme at the top of the texture, before closing with a return to the semiquaver ostinato in the cello.

(3) Menuetto and Trio. Allegro

K.465's Minuet is another example of miniature sonata form. The first section is subdivided into irregular phrase-lengths of $4 + 2 + 5$ [$= 1 + 4$] $+ 5 + 4$ bars, and introduces several distinct thematic elements defined as much by rhythm and phrasing as by intervallic content. The textures shift rapidly from phrase to phrase, encompassing tune-and-accompaniment, unison, and fully fledged counterpoint. Following the opening theme (bars 1–4) is a contrasting unison pattern, *forte*, out of which the third element (bars 6–11) grows, resetting the unison figure in the first violin above a contrasting countertheme and evolving a new invertible suffix (bar 8) woven contrapuntally through the entire ensemble as far as the D major 7th *sforzando* in bar 12; this resolves four bars later in the dominant, G, at which point a closing theme featuring slurred quaver pairs over a light crotchet accompaniment is introduced.

In the second section new environments appear all the time, much as in a sonata-form development. These include a chromatically modified unison statement of the opening theme (bars 20^3–24); melodic restatement over a pedal (bar 24^3ff.); theme-as-bass (bar 27^3ff.); texture inversion (bar 32ff.); voice-pairs (bar 36ff.); and contrapuntal imitation (bar 39ff.) – this last covering the recapitulation of the opening theme. Eventually, the closing theme is richly repeated, *forte*.

Within the Trio (likewise influenced by sonata planning, with a recapitulation in the cello at bars 28–9) there is a far greater degree of phrase symmetry. Its first eight bars consist of balancing phrases, a norm which is continued in the imitative dialogue of bars 9–12, extended sequentially after the double-bar, and finally crowned in the last twelve bars by the textural inversion in which the cello takes up the theme (which serves perfectly well as a bass line). The 'development' begins by inverting the opening theme and concludes (bars 25–8) with a reference back to the canonic procedure of bars 9–12, this time over a preparatory dominant pedal.

(4) Allegro molto

The finale is a lively contredanse in sonata form (exposition, bars 1–136; development, bars 136–98; recapitulation, bars 199–371; coda, bars 371–419). Its phrases unfold in strongly periodic fashion and with almost relentless energy, establishing a regularity which Mozart upsets in various ways, the most obvious of which is silence. On no fewer than nine occasions the main theme is abruptly broken off by rests, in a witty Haydnesque manner, after which the preceding momentum is regained. Apart from such straightforward dislocation Mozart injects the necessary element of contrast by means of register contrast, flexibility of texture and tonal digression.

An early illustration of the effectiveness of even a brief opposition of register and dynamic occurs at bars 16–17 and 20–1 (the *forte* interjections); others include the contrast of *piano* and *forte* dynamics in bar 34 and the *forte* outburst at bar 162. Textural contrast is present throughout the finale. The second subject at bar 54, for instance, reduces the texture to just two strands of neatly articulated counterpoint – a welcome relief from the wide leaps and full-bodied semiquaver *tremolandi* characteristic of the preceding transition (bars 34–53). Following a restatement in full four-part texture is a concertante passage for the solo first violin, lightly accompanied by the rest of the ensemble and ending with alternate loud–soft cadential progressions (bars 83–7) confirming the dominant key.

Unexpected tonal shifts provide another means of contrast. At bar 89 Mozart interrupts the flow of his second-subject group with a new octave theme in E flat, winding chromatically back to G at bar 103 for the exposition's closing paragraph. This introduces a new figure of three repeated quavers and a falling fifth (bars 125–6) featuring, like the first subject, a prominent upbeat; this is subsequently taken up in the development. Further tonal contrast is provided by commencing a tonic-minor statement of the first subject, breaking off at bar 150 and resuming (fragmented) in E flat in bars 151–2 before turning to the closing motif (bars 125–6) in stretto. This alternates at first with fragments of the main theme in the first violin before taking over the texture entirely (sometimes inverted) in bars 160–80. From bar 165

Mozart modulates rapidly by circle-of-fifths motion through E minor, B minor, F sharp minor, C sharp minor, G sharp minor ('keys' which are briefly established by their own dominants, and then immediately passed over), concluding (bar 180) with V/E major, by which time all sense of the home key and its close relatives has been undermined. The harmonic audacity of this development section anticipates that in the finale of the G minor Symphony K.550, completed some three-and-a-half years later. Following three fragmentary attempts at a false recapitulation of the main theme in E major/minor, the true recapitulation begins in bar 199. Mozart's deflation of the harmonic tension in this retransition, gradually fanning-out the span of the staccato contrary motion scales across the whole of the ensemble in bars 192–8, is masterly in its simplicity and economy of means.

Within the recapitulation the main departure from the exposition is the expansion of bars 89–103 (the E flat interruption of the second-subject group) at bars 292–326. First appearing in A flat, the new theme reappears in dialogue between the outer parts in D flat (bar 308), regaining the tonic, C, via a chromatic ascent to the dominant, G, in the bass (bar 318ff.) for the concertante passage with which the section culminates. To counterbalance the harmonic extremities of the development (and perhaps also the very recent digression into flat keys), Mozart appends an extended coda which returns to the opening theme (bar 371) and confirms the tonic, C, with a series of strong cadential gestures culminating in a written-out trill for all four instruments and some new melodic strands, ending with a final reprise of the quaver pattern from the end of the exposition.

5

Some theoretical perspectives

Whereas Chapter 4 provides an overview of individual quartets, this chapter offers particular theoretical perspectives on selected movements, or sections of movements, drawing upon eighteenth-century theories of rhetoric and topicality.

Mozart himself wrote no textbooks, nor is he known to have subscribed to any one particular branch of the theoretical investigation of music. His father, however, maintained a keen interest in theoretical issues and owned a number of textbooks by Fux, Mattheson and Riepel. He even told Mozart that he intended one day to write a theoretical work of his own.[1] It is unlikely that Mozart was ignorant of eighteenth-century music theory, however silent he remained about it in his correspondence.

The objectives of this chapter are to illustrate some ways in which Mozart's quartets might have been appreciated by late eighteenth-century musicians within some prevailing theoretical frameworks; and to allow for more extensive treatment of some aspects of individual movements than is possible or appropriate in the preceding synopsis.

Rhetorical approaches

The belief that musical form was analogous to rhetoric was by no means uncommon during the eighteenth century. Johann Nikolaus Forkel applied the accepted divisions of an oration to the analysis of musical form as follows:

> one of the main points in musical rhetoric and aesthetics is the ordering of musical ideas and the progression of the sentiments expressed through them, so that these ideas are conveyed to our hearts with a certain coherence, just as the ideas in an oration are conveyed to our

minds and follow one another according to logical principles. When ordered in an appropriate manner, these elements are thus to the language of sentiments the equivalent of that which in the language of ideas ... are the well-known elements still preserved by good, genuine orators – that is *exordium, propositio, refutatio, confirmatio,* etc.[2]

A musical 'oration', according to Forkel, consisted of the following three distinct stages:

(i) *Erfindung* – the creation of basic melodic ideas.

(ii) *Ausführung* (or *Anordnung*) – the planning of the movement, in which the basic ideas of the *Erfindung* are arranged into a coherent order.

(iii) *Ausarbeitung* – the actual composition of the movement, in which the fine detail of the themes, harmonies, phrases, periods, etc., are worked out.

Forkel's observations relate to the first three of the five *partes* of an oration – Invention (*inventio*), Arrangement (*dispositio*) and Style (*elocutio*) – as described by such ancient classical authors as Cicero and Quintilian, on whose work eighteenth-century rhetorical writing was based.[3] These were the technical and practical means by which an oration was structured. The second category, Arrangement, was typically divided into six parts – Introduction (*exordium*), Statement of facts (*narratio*), Proposition (*propositio*), Proof (*confirmatio*), Refutation (*disputatio*) and Conclusion (*peroratio*) – and it is to these that Forkel compares the 'rhetorical' subdivisions of musical form in the first of his comments quoted above.[4]

❧ There is good reason to believe that Leopold Mozart was interested in rhetoric. Before writing his treatise on violin playing, *Versuch einer gründliche Violinschule* (Augsburg, 1756),[5] he devoted himself to the study of rhetorical textbooks. On 9 June and again on 28 August 1755 he wrote to the Augsburg publisher Johann Jakob Lotter requesting copies of the works of the rhetorician and lexicographer Johann Christoph Gottsched, perhaps on the recommendation of Gottsched's one-time pupil Lorenz Mizler, editor of the Leipzig periodical *Neueröffnete musikalische Bibliothek* (1739–54), to which Leopold was a subscriber.[6]

Rhetoric affords us an interesting perspective on some compositional features of Mozart's quartets. *Inventio* (Forkel's *Erfindung*) applies most obviously to a movement's principal thematic material, the stuff of 'inspiration'. In the Andante con moto of K.428, the finale of K.465, or the slow-movement variations of K.464, for instance, the 'inspiration' was clearly melodic. Alternatively, *inventio* may be as much harmonic as melodic, as at the opening of K.421 which features a prominent descending chaconne-like tetrachord, D–A, in the bass. Harmonic *inventio* is naturally not confined to openings of movements but can encompass such harmonically driven passages as the development of K.421's first movement, starting out from E flat (bar 42) and heading towards A minor (bar 46); or the culminating cadential gesture in bars 34–40 of the opening Allegro non troppo of K.428, strongly spiced by the chromatic augmented-sixth chord, *crescendo*, at bar 37. The initial harmonic conception of a transition or development belongs properly to the level of *inventio*, while its precise ordering (that is, the co-ordination of the underlying harmonic steps with the thematic material) belongs to the subsequent stage of *dispositio* (Forkel's *Ausführung*). For example, in the first-movement exposition of the A major quartet K.464 the transition from 'first subject' to 'second subject' consists of a shift to the tonic minor at bar 9, leading on to the relative major, C (bar 13), which, eventually heightened by extension to an augmented-sixth chord at bar 20, prepares for the strong arrival of the B major chord at bar 21, the 'local dominant' degree, resolving to E major at bar 25 (the 'second subject'). This basic progression is the *inventio*. The actual articulation of the stages in this harmonic unfolding is achieved by adaptation of the opening theme to a contrapuntal texture (bar 9), a new theme (C major), and a stabilising cadential progression emphasising B at the end: all technical processes that belong to the next-highest rhetorical level, *dispositio*.

Forkel's subdivisions (*Erfindung*, *Ausführung*, *Ausarbeitung*) tempt us to view the successive stages in the genesis of a musical work in such conceptually separated terms: first the invention (the stuff of 'inspiration'), next the technical 'fleshing out'. However, the matter is not quite so unambiguous. Quintilian's discussion of *inventio*[7] dwells upon the relationship between invention and judgement ('it is necessary first to invent and then to exercise our judgement'); the fact that this comment occurs before he turns his attention to *dispositio* implies

Ex. 5.1 Cancelled version of K.464, first movement, bar 107ff.

that in oratory some preliminary reflection on the *inventio* was una-voidable and that the dividing line between invention and ordering was sometimes a fine one.

This is true equally of musical composition. The ambiguity is well illustrated by the autograph of the first movement of K.464. Mozart's first draft of the passage beginning at bar 107 continued as shown in Example 5.1, which shows that the original harmonic *inventio* pro-longed the G major seventh chord throughout the first seven bars (including the unsupported second-violin phrase). The change of har-monic direction in the finished version, which moves sharpwards to a cadence on C sharp (V/ F sharp) in bar 118, represents an adaptation of the original *inventio* to the detailed tonal and formal characteristics of the *dispositio*. But where the former ends and the latter begins is impossible to tell. Nor is this the only case of 'second thoughts' in these quartets. As we have seen in Chapter 2, Mozart's initial idea for the opening bars of K.458's finale was to present the main theme in an imitative context, though he decided instead to delay this until the development section – a clear example of the adaptation of his original *inventio* to serve a rather different formal purpose (*dispositio*). Mozart 'invented' and subsequently 'exercised his judgement', deferring immediate contrapuntal treatment for the sake of the broader structure.

Another way of treating the relationship between Forkel's three levels of *Erfindung*, *Ausführung* and *Ausarbeitung* is as a 'background model' behind an actual theme – a basic pattern (which may be either melodic or harmonic) constituting the actual 'inspiration' which the composer subsequently elaborated. Such distinctions were commonplace in the compositional pedagogy of Mozart's time and provide a useful adjunct to rhetorical understanding of melody and its elaboration.

For example, eighteenth-century treatises frequently make a distinction between *simple* melody and *figured* melody. The latter builds upon the former, resulting in melodic decoration of a simple underlying pattern – one that could legitimately be traced back to the species counterpoint demonstrations in Fux's *Gradus ad Parnassum* (Vienna, 1725).[8] It is incorporated in a number of eighteenth-century treatises to varying degrees, the most extreme being Koch's *Versuch einer Anleitung zur Composition* (Leipzig, 1782–93)[9] in which a simple eight-bar melody is extended into an entire movement of thirty-two bars entirely by melodic decoration and repetition.[10]

An illustration of the relationship between simple and figured melody is provided by the slow movement of K.465, bars 13–23. The dialogue between the first violin and cello (and latterly, the inner parts, too) is a simple decoration of the underlying harmonic progression shown in Example 5.2a. A similar approach is found in the slow movement of K.458, beginning at bar 21, in which the embellishment is still more pronounced (Ex. 5.2b). The exposition transition in the first movement of K.428 (bars 21–5) can be regarded as an elaboration of a more basic upper neighbour plus falling scale-progression (Ex. 5.2c).

Melodic embellishment (such as that at bar 45ff. of the slow movement of K.465, decorating the reprise of the opening theme) is a compositional practice that resides within the third of Forkel's rhe-

Ex. 5.2a Hypothetical reduction of K.465, second movement, bars 13–23

Ex. 5.2b Melodic reductions of K.458, second movement, bars 21³–25¹

Ex. 5.2c Melodic reduction of K.428, first movement, bars 16–24

torical levels, the *Ausarbeitung*. While this level was primarily concerned with the 'refinements' of melody and harmony (the judicious application of certain well-known *figures* – turns, trills, expressive appoggiaturas and so on), it influenced the design of movements to no small degree since figures of embellishment are inextricably bound up with the repetition of patterns which, in turn, have an effect on the larger structures in which they are placed. Such figures play a central role in the composition of variations and episodic forms.

Fundamental to the design of any set of variations is the principle of progressive embellishment of the original theme. Elaine Sisman, in her thoroughly absorbing study of Haydn's variations, has developed a rhetorical model to account for this, based on techniques borrowed from the classical textbook *Ad Herrenium*.[11] Sisman takes the rhetorical figure of 'Refining' (*expolitio*), 'dwelling on the same topic and yet seeming to say something ever new', either repeating the same idea, or successively elaborating upon it. An alternative rhetorical device, perhaps more widely applicable to variations, is the *trope*, likewise discussed by the author of *Ad Herrenium*[12] and, in greater detail, by Quintilian (*Institutio Oratoria*, VIII.vi), who describes it as 'the artistic alteration of a word or phrase from its proper meaning to another' (*Institutio*, VIII.vi.1–3). For Quintilian, the most important trope was the *metaphor*, in which 'an object … is actually substituted for the thing [we wish to describe]'.[13] Applied to variation movements, each of the variations on the theme may be regarded as a metaphor of that theme (a new term 'substituted' for it and exercising a kind of 'commentary' on it), strictly maintaining its original phraseology and, with the occasional exception, harmonic structure.

The analogy of the metaphor accounts for the unfolding narrative of Mozart's variations on at least two levels. On the melodic level, the first violin's continuous demisemiquavers in variation 1 of K.464's Andante are a metaphor for the theme, although, typically for Mozart, the melodic contour of the original is heavily disguised even at this early stage. Some essentials are retained, however. The element of syncopation in bar 1 of the theme is enhanced at bar 19 by upward transposition of the F sharp, its value shortened to a tied quaver interrupting what is otherwise a continuous flow of demisemiquavers. In variation 3 Mozart marks this syncopation still more pointedly, the viola's entries on top D (bar 55) and E (bar 57) juxtaposed antiphonally against the preceding violin pair. In texture, too, metaphor operates in this movement: in variations 3–5 each successive dialogue (see the synopsis of this movement in Chapter 4) is a metaphor of its predecessor, lending a sense of formal coherence to the centre of the movement.

Topicality in the first movement of K.458

Topical associations represent a dimension of meaning for the music of Mozart's time that was almost wholly lost during the nineteenth and twentieth centuries, and which has only in recent times regained the attention of musicologists, most especially Leonard Ratner.[14] 'Topics' were recognisable 'codes' according to which music was both composed and understood and thus provided a context for communication between the composer, the performer and the listener in the classical period – a kind of musical vernacular. According to Wye J. Allanbrook, the composer had at his fingertips 'an expressive vocabulary, a collection in music of what in the theory of rhetoric are called *topoi*, or topics for formal discourse ... held in common with his audience ... each musical *topos* has associations both natural and historical, which can be expressed in words, and which were tacitly shared by the eighteenth–century audience'.[15] On the one hand, topics could include dance metres of various sorts (the first movement of K.464, for example, captures the idiom of the minuet, while the slow movement of K.465 might be regarded as a sarabande). On the other, topics embrace idioms such as the so-called 'brilliant style' – virtuoso runs of semiquavers – as found in the finales of K.428, bars 90–104, and K.465, bars 69–86, for instance; *Sturm und Drang* – a style of heightened emotional expression featuring audacious melodic, harmonic and rhythmic devices, wide interval leaps, disjunction of *Affekt* in successive phrases, and predominantly minor mode – as in the first movement of K.421, or the sudden outbursts in the finale K.465 (bars 39–53);[16] and 'learned counterpoint' – a device found in very different contexts in the finales of K.387 and K.464. Considerable portions of movements may be accounted for by a succession of topics. The first-movement exposition of K.465 contains several contrasting topics: a vocal 'cantabile' style (bars 23–30); 'learned counterpoint' (bars 44–50); and 'brilliant' or 'virtuoso' style (bars 56–71 and 84–91). As Agawu has convincingly shown, the characteristics of individual topics are not necessarily mutually exclusive but can profitably overlap because of shared subsidiary characteristics. Within K.458's first movement, for example, the 'hunting' topic takes place within a 6/8 metre, a 'neutral' parameter that can support other characteristics, such as the 'brilliant' style (bar 11ff.) and the 'learned counterpoint' that rises to its peak in the coda (bar 239ff.).[17]

For composers, as for orators, topics were 'sources' from which usable material might be drawn; for the listener, topics provided a reference point, a kind of 'grid' through which to sift the music into recognisable patterns. Topics might usefully be regarded as a common stock of suitable types of music to be applied in certain situations. For composers of baroque opera, whose guiding principle was the doctrine of the *Affekt*, a working knowledge of topics was essential to the representation of particular actions and feelings through suitable music (pastoral, festive, warlike, and so on).[18] Such topical 'sources of arguments' were well known to the young Mozart who, as recorded by Daines Barrington in 1769, could improvise a 'Song of Rage' at will, no doubt utilising a particular 'fingerprint' or group of associated fingerprints, such as tremolando figures, minor triads, dislocation of register, and so on.[19]

Recognition of appropriate 'topics' can affect our appreciation of even the most familiar music. At an early stage in its history the B flat quartet, K.458, acquired the nickname 'Jagd' ('Hunt') because of its opening 'hunting call' in 6/8 metre. The name did not derive from Mozart – neither the autograph nor the Artaria first edition bears any trace of such a title, which can only be explained by association with the well-known eighteenth-century 'topic' of the 'chasse'. For Mozart's contemporaries, the first movement of K.458 evidently evoked the 'chasse' topic, the main components of which were 6/8 tempo (sometimes featuring a strong upbeat) and triadic melodies based largely around the tonic and dominant chords (doubtless stemming from the physical limitation of the actual hunting horn to notes of the harmonic series).[20] Alexander Ringer has remarked that the 'hunting' association in this movement appears to reside almost exclusively in its 6/8 tempo and that the nickname 'Hunt' is therefore largely inappropriate to this piece.[21]

In fact, the 'chasse' topic affects the movement rather more than Ringer admits. Its opening melody, which recurs quite often, is clearly triadic; so is the theme at bars 41–2; so, in outline, is the theme at bars 54–5; likewise the new theme with which the development opens. Other 'chasse' characteristics include the extremely regular periodicity (and especially the tendency at the opening towards short phrases, punctuated by frequent cadences), outlining symmetrical four-bar phrase units which avoid elision to a degree unusual in Mozart's music at this stage in his development, and the quantity of imitation (an important additional connotation of 'chasse', in which one part, quite literally, 'chases' another). There is both thematic and textural imitation here: thematic at bars 42–6, 125–7, 130–3 and the frequent stretto devices of the coda (bars 230–79); textural, as at bars 54–66, in which the restatement of the material of bars 54–60 in bars 60–6 is in effect an imitation of a low tessitura group by a high tessitura group, and bars 77–90, in which an antiphonal dialogue is set up between the two inner voices and the solo first violin, over a pedal bass.

Antiphony is a device that accounts for a significant proportion of the development, too: the tonal progression from F minor (bar 106) to E flat (bar 125) is articulated by a textural progression from a solo–accompaniment of the new theme at bar 106 towards a more thoroughly integrated imitative exchange from bar 118. But at this stage we have probably reached the point at which imitation and its textural extensions act purely as a metaphor for the 'chasse' topic. Thematically, the outline is no longer triadic, but is supplanted by both a more chromatic profile and a greater flexibility of note-values, encompassing busy semiquavers and legato dotted crotchets. So many different expressive elements compete for our attention in this passage that any trace of the 'pure' topic has been lost.

Interestingly, the beginning of this passage, bar 106, is precisely the point in his autograph at which Mozart apparently interrupted composition of this quartet in summer 1783 (bar 106 to the end of the movement were eventually completed in a different ink-colour, see Chapter 2 above). Up to the start of bar 106, and including the overtly triadic opening of the development section, the 'chasse' topic remains a significant issue. From bar 106, on the other hand, it becomes far less prominent. Starting in bar 134, triadic thematic elements, clearly related to bars 42ff. of the exposition, sneak back into the texture in counterpoint beneath a continuation of the legato dotted crotchets that had gradually risen to prominence during the preceding thirty bars, finally giving way once again to a return of the initial 'hunt' motif at the point of recapitulation. According to this interpretation, much of the development section does not 'fit' with the 'chasse' topic of the exposition, and a marked discontinuity results.

Discontinuity is not the same thing as incoherence, however, and, for all the appearance of a fractured surface, there is a rhetorical sense in which bars 106–25 'belong' to bars 1–106. When he resumed work on K.458 in autumn 1784 (his 'Verzeichnüss' bears the completion date of 9 November) Mozart must have examined the extant portion of the movement to remind himself of its content and to look for potential features for development. That is, he would have moved from the rhetorical level of *inventio*, particular features of exposition material, to the level of *dispositio*, on which he would work out that material's potential. One such feature is the flexibility with which the theme at bars 41–2 is subsequently handled: in bars 47–50 it sheds its two-note upbeat, beginning instead with the prominent four-semiquaver group in canon between first violin and viola over a chromatically enhanced pedal C; in bars 51–2 it is transplanted into a solo-accompaniment context over punctuating quaver chords; in bars 54–65 it retains the solo–accompaniment context but grows a new three-note upbeat and acquires legato support; and finally bar 66 returns to the scansion of bar 51, but within a richer contrapuntal framework. At each stage, the four-semiquaver figure is present, though its precise location, and therefore scansion within the 6/8 bar, shifts. This procedure is analogous to one of the so-called rhetorical tropes, *hyperbaton*, which Quintilian defines as 'the transposition of a word' by which he means either simple reversal in the normal order of two words (a stylistic figure) or an adaptation of the norm in the interests of structure.[22] Mozart's procedure in bars 41–70 clearly serves a structural rather than an ornamental purpose, as there is a sense in which this passage evolves towards a goal. Each successive stage in these thirty bars presents a further development of the four-semiquaver pattern. Rhetorically, the *inventio* comprises the four-semiquaver pattern, the *dispositio* the technical means by which Mozart transforms its thematic and textural contexts. The development takes this process a stage further. Here it is the texture which continually shifts, beginning with the simplicity of the offbeat quaver chord accompaniment at bar 106 and culminating, via a steady progression through enhanced antiphonal dialogue, in the canonic work from bar 125 to bar 134. Thematically, bars 106–37, described above, feature a four-semiquaver group that could quite convincingly be interpreted as a further evolution of the figure at bars 41–2; moreover, given the gradually increasing complexity of the antiphonal texture, the arrival of the canon at bar 126 is a carefully prepared *climax*, a well-known rhetorical device.[23]

To summarise: Mozart's development section begins with a continuation of the 'chasse' topic (bars 90–106), departs from that topic's overt characteristics in order to explore a subsidiary agenda of transformation (bars 106–25), and finally reintegrates the 'chasse' by means of a clearly stated thematic 'fingerprint' (bars 125–6 and, especially, bars 130–7 over a dominant pedal, preparing for the recapitulation) that signals the return of the original topic. The presence or absence of the 'chasse' topic provides a framework for the understanding of this movement independent of its tonal functions. Its form is created in a very important sense by topical discontinuity.

6

Reception of the 'Haydn' quartets

Early editions and copies

The continued popularity of Mozart's quartets after his death is confirmed to some extent by the number of new editions (or reissues of older ones) that appeared until well into the nineteenth century before the inauguration of the Breitkopf and Härtel *Gesamtausgabe W. A. Mozarts Werke* in 1877.[1] Many editions or reissues appeared between 1791 and *c*. 1830 in Vienna, Paris, London, Offenbach-am-Main, Cologne and Leipzig. Most of these were issued in playing parts, although scores were also made available by Johann Traeg (Vienna) in 1804[2] and Ignaz Pleyel (Paris) in 1807–8.[3] Typically these were printed in two volumes, each containing three quartets, though the order of pieces does not always follow that of the Artaria first edition.[4] Frequently some special authority was claimed for a particular edition: Imbault, for example, noted on the title-page of his 'Nouvelle Edition' of *c*. 1809[5] that it was 'Faite d'après l'Edition Originale de Vienne', whereas André, who had purchased many of Mozart's autographs from Constanze in November 1799, proudly announced that his text [6] was 'faite d'après le manuscrit original de l'auteur'.

The fact that some publishers issued the works more than once (Sieber and Pleyel in Paris, André in Offenbach, Lavenu in London) shows that, for publishers, Mozart's quartets continued to be valuable commodities. The proliferation of published arrangements of the quartets for other instruments reinforces this: versions for woodwind and strings, piano solo, piano duet, two pianos and even full orchestra appeared in the early nineteenth century.[7] One English edition, produced by Clementi and Collard & Collard some time between 1810 and 1818,[8] made prominent reference to the fact that it was 'Respectfully Dedicated by Permission To His Royal Highness The Prince of

Wales' – a sign of Royal approval that would not be lost on prospective purchasers.

Among the large number of early manuscript copies of the quartets are two in Beethoven's hand, one of the whole of K.387 and another of K.464's Andante. Both manuscripts are thought to date from about 1800.[9]

Early critical reactions

Among the earliest critical reactions to Mozart's 'Haydn' quartets was a comment in Heinrich Christoph Koch's *Versuch einer Anleitung zur Composition* (1793) to the effect that these works were praiseworthy for 'their special mixture of the strict and free styles and the treatment of harmony'.[10] By 'mixture of strict and free styles' Koch was perhaps referring to the finale of K.387, although his comment could apply more generally given the flexibility with which Mozart integrates counterpoint with galant elements throughout this set. It is nevertheless interesting that Koch should single out this conjunction of styles as something positive, since in his treatise he deplored the fact that in the late eighteenth century fugue was appreciated 'in an instrumental work only when it is combined with comic ornaments in one and the same movement to provoke laughter. Now so many amateurs of the art wish to have such compositions, many composers, indeed, serve them up.'

According to Professor Lorenz Hübner, the editor of the *Salzburger Zeitung* from 1784, favourable reports of the quartets had appeared in Berlin newspapers soon after their publication. He told Leopold:

> It is really astonishing to see what a number of compositions your son is publishing. In all the announcement of musical works I see nothing but Mozart. The Berlin announcements, when quoting the quartets, merely add the following words: 'It is quite unnecessary to recommend these quartets to the public. Suffice it to say that they are the work of Herr Mozart.'[11]

In some quarters, what Haydn called Mozart's 'profound knowledge of composition' was felt to be a disadvantage. A report in Cramer's *Magasin der Musik* (23 April 1787) described Mozart as the most skilful and best keyboard player I have ever heard; the only pity is that he aims too high in his artful and truly beautiful compositions, in order to be a new creator, whereby it must be said that feeling and heart profit little; his new Quartets for two violins, viola and bass, which he has dedicated to Haydn, may well be called too highly seasoned – and whose palate can endure this for long?[12]

Apparently Cramer believed that the prolonged intensity of Mozart's music was sometimes a barrier to widespread popular appreciation. It confounded traditional expectations (of periodicity, for instance), making demands that its listeners were not prepared to accept. While compositional artfulness was to be admired, it was not to be overdone either; intervening passages of a simple nature were required between virtuoso displays of counterpoint, or motivic development. Incredible as it may seem, some of Mozart's contemporaries felt that his quartets lacked such passages,[13] progressing at too high a level of artfulness for too long. Cramer does not specify a particular quartet or movement that he felt was 'too highly seasoned', though candidates are not hard to find. Possible examples include the 'dissonant' Adagio of K.465, the ghostly chromatic opening of K.428, and the Trio of K.387. In the first-movement development section of K.464, the almost unrelieved density of the contrapuntal texture may perhaps have left some eighteenth-century listeners exhausted. The Minuet of K.428 is likewise quite demanding of the listener, involving a theme whose opening (minus the unsupported first bar plus upbeat) soon returns as a closing cadential device (bars 10–14; and again at bars 30–4); in the second section this theme is used in stretto against itself, with entries in the viola (bar 22), first violin (bar 24) and cello (bar 26). Still more demanding, perhaps, is the ensuing Trio, certainly in terms of its chromaticism and phrase-structure. Appreciating such shifting perspectives requires unfailing attention – something not every eighteenth-century listener was prepared to give, it seems.[14]

Early nineteenth-century 'narrativity'

The first movement of Mozart's D minor quartet K.421 was taken by Jérome-Joseph Momigny as the basis of an extended musical analysis in his *Cours Complet d'Harmonie et de Composition* (1806).[15] Momigny quotes the whole movement as a musical example, including, in addition to the four quartet staves, various 'explanatory staves' showing melodic and harmonic reductions, a setting of the principal melodic part for voice (to a text chosen by Momigny) with accompaniment conflated from the quartet texture, and a 'fundamental bass' – a figured chordal reduction of the harmonic progressions to their underlying root-position chords. Momigny's analysis is an impressive demonstration of phrase-divisions, cadence-structure and harmonic grammar, but his primary purpose is to convey the expressive qualities of Mozart's music. The text was chosen to suit Momigny's interpretation of the *Affekt* of this movement:

> I believed that the sentiments expressed by the composer were those of
> a lover on the point of being abandoned by the hero whom she loves;
> *Dido*, who suffered such a misfortune, came immediately to my mind.
> Her lofty station, the ardour of her love, the familiarity of her misfor-
> tune, all these persuaded me to make her the heroine of this subject.[16]

While Momigny's detailed attention to elements of motivic, harmonic, periodic and tonal grammar is in itself worthy of study as an example of early nineteenth-century analytical thinking, the main feature from the point of view of reception is that, for Momigny, this music evoked powerful emotional associations. It expressed a train of narrative thought, which Momigny brought alive by the addition of a particular programme, and through which he sought to represent Mozart's style to his readers. The first movement of K.421 encapsulated for him a particular set of sentiments; it could be 'read' as a story. Momigny's 'narrative' analysis suggests unsuspected layers of interpretation lost during the remainder of the nineteenth and twentieth centuries.

Fétis and the Adagio of K.465

The puzzling chromaticism of the opening of the 'Dissonance' quartet K.465 prompted vigorous discussion in the scholarly musical literature of the late 1820s and early 1830s. Fétis, in particular, devoted much attention to the Adagio in his journal *La Revue musicale*, believing that Mozart could not have intended such dissonance. In July 1829 he produced a study of these bars in which he printed a revision of his own, to stand comparison with the alleged misprint of Mozart's intentions in all available editions.[17] This provoked a dispute with François-Louis Perne, whose objections to Fétis's revision were printed in the journal the following month, together with a response from Fétis himself.[18] Fétis returned to this subject again in July 1830 with an extended discussion incorporating some new 'Observations sur l'analyse du Quatuor op.10 en *ut* majeur par A. C. Leduc dans l'*Allgemeine musikalische Zeitung* de Leipzig'.[19] This comprised an introduction to the problem, a resolution proposed by Fétis taken from his *Traité de contrepoint et fugue* (Paris, 1824) and an alternative harmonic resolution by Leduc. The German musical journal *Cäcilia* attempted the most thorough review of this issue in 1832.[20] Stretching over nearly fifty pages, it offered a series of quotations of comments by Haydn (who is said to have remarked that 'if this is what Mozart wrote, then this is what Mozart meant'), Giuseppe Sarti,[21] Fétis, Perne and Leduc, together with an overview of the theoretical and tonal frameworks of the Adagio by Gottfried Weber, in a sincere attempt to account for its harmonic audacities in terms of contemporary music theory, including Daniel Gottlob Türk's *Kurze Anweisung zum Generalbass-spielen*.[22] Selections from this debate were reprinted in the London periodical *The Harmonicon*,[23] including extracts from Sarti's venomous attack, although at the end of the article the (anonymous) compiler was careful to explain that Sarti's comments were the product of jealousy at Mozart's success as an opera composer in Milan in the early 1770s. Sarti's main objection to the opening of K.465 concerned false relations, for example of A flat and A natural in bar 2 ('a most execrable commencement') and such chromatic extremes as the A sharp/F juxtaposition in bars 20–1 ('most miserable in an Adagio'). Likewise offensive to Sarti was the development section of K.421's first movement, which he quotes for purposes of comparison, principally such harmonic features as the prolonged dissonance A/B flat in bar 54 (logical in its imitative context, of course) which 'offends the ear by its long continuance ... From [such] examples it may be perceived that the author (whom I neither know nor wish to know) is nothing more than a piano-forte player with spoiled ears, who does not concern himself about counterpoint.'[24]

A brief resumé of the debate over K.465 was given by Otto Jahn in

1856. Jahn's account of Mozart's chamber music includes a section on the 'Haydn' quartets that epitomises the musical criticism of its age, profoundly influenced, as Jahn himself admits, by Beethoven and dominated by thematic constructions of form. At times Jahn's discussion tends towards the picturesque. Of K.465 he notes that it reveals 'that higher peace to which a noble mind attains through strife and suffering ... [its Andante is] one of those wonderful manifestations of genius which are only of the earth in so far as they take effect upon human minds; which soar aloft into a region of blessedness where suffering and passion are transfigured'.[25] Jahn's contextual introduction to the quartets is in itself an interesting early example of *Rezeptionsgeschichte*, for he is careful to distinguish contemporary (that is, mid-nineteenth-century) views from earlier attitudes. For example, Jahn reports an alleged conversation between Dittersdorf and Emperor Joseph II in 1786 in which, asked to draw a comparison between Haydn and Mozart, the composer replied with a telling poetic analogy to the effect that Mozart was music's Klopstock, whereas Haydn was music's Gellert:

> whereupon Joseph replied that both were great poets, but that Klopstock must be read repeatedly in order to understand his beauties, whereas Gellert's beauties lay plainly exposed to the first glance ... However odd may appear to us [in the 1850s] – admiring as we do, above all things in Mozart, his clearness and purity of form – Dittersdorf's comparison of him with Klopstock, it is nevertheless instructive, as showing that his contemporaries prized his grandeur and dignity, and the force and boldness of his expression, as his highest and most distinguishing qualities.[26]

Twentieth-century approaches

Unity and variety: Hans Keller

One significant trend in twentieth-century musical criticism has been the attempt to represent movements or even whole works as a kind of organism, growing 'naturally' out of fundamental material. Among the most prominent of such critics was Hans Keller, whose quest to trace the latent unity behind a surface variety sprang from his acquaintance with Freudian psycho-analysis:

> a great piece grows from an all-embracing idea. Great music diversifies a unity; mere good music unifies diverse elements ... The oneness, the simultaneity is the inner reality, the Kantian thing-in-itself, the Schopenhauerian will, the Freudian unconscious (which is essentially timeless), while the temporal succession is its necessary appearance, the Schopenhauerian idea, the Freudian conscious. Thus experienced, *variety is the necessary means of expressing a unity* that would otherwise remain unexpressed...[27]

Mozart's chamber music was one of Keller's enduring passions and in *The Mozart Companion* (1956) he turned his attention to the 'Haydn' quartets. Something of the complexity of his approach is revealed in the discussion of part of the exposition of the first movement of the G major quartet K.387, an approach which, however controversial it may appear, truly engages with Mozart's music in an attempt to uncover a single focus for this blatantly polythematic piece:

> The melodic evolution of K.387 in G (1787 [*recte* 1782]) immediately shows both the master and the genius; every note is over-determined, and everything springs from the basic motif (x).

K.387, first movement – opening theme with Keller's bracketed annotations

> The basic fourth is at once reversed and filled up scale-wise (x¹), in which basic shape it serves as main thematic material. The first half of the second bar represents, in diminution, a retrograde version of the first bar, while the cadential motif of its second half is a straight (con) sequence of the first bar's second half, and just as a semitone is here replaced by a whole tone, a whole tone has been replaced by a semitone in the four-quaver motif. X¹ appears in straight form in the second half of the third bar, but in the first half it develops towards what is ultimately to become the second subject. The shake itself increases the oscillating motion that is to become the characteristic rhythmic feature of the subsidiary theme [the second subject, bar 27]; whereas the semi-

quaver diminution of x[1] establishes the actual rhythm of this feature, whose notes (mediant and sharpened supertonic) come from bar 4's cadential motif, itself a crab of x[1]'s cadential notes (g^2– f sharp[2]) ... The fundamental motif of the consequent (bar 5) introduces a rhythmic variation of x (minus upbeat) plus x[1], and further develops the forthcoming second subject's semiquaver rhythm. [28]

The reception of 'influence': Haydn's quartets and Mozart's 'Haydn' quartets

The question of Haydn's influence on these quartets is inescapable. Existing accounts of the 'Haydn' quartets frequently stress their relationship to Haydn's most recently published set, Op. 33 (1781–2). In Stanley Sadie's opinion, 'The Mozart set shows a definite debt to op. 33 in the way important material is often given to the inner parts and in the generally concentrated style ... one can demonstrate Mozart's familiarity with the Haydn quartets by their echoes, no doubt subconscious, in his own: Mozart's 6/8 variation finale in K.421 is indebted to Haydn's in [Op. 33] no. 5, while the openings of the minuets in the two E flat quartets (K.428 and no. 2) are markedly alike.'[29] In the accounts of Einstein and Wyzewa and Saint-Foix, a similar relationship is claimed.[30]

It cannot be denied that the rhythm and phraseology of the finale of K.421 bears a strong affinity to that of Haydn's G major quartet op. 33 no. 5. Other similarities exist between the first movements of K.458 and Haydn's Op. 33 no. 6, between the chromaticism of K.387's finale and the first movement of Haydn's Op. 33 no. 1 (bars 54–64), and between the slow movements of K.465 and Op. 33 no. 3 (both are F major movements in 3/4 time, are of cantabile character, and exhibit similar approaches to phrasing and melodic embellishment).

Influence, though, is about more than incidental thematic or formal resemblances. It can be as much about transformation as replication of an earlier composer's ideas. A recent study of these quartets by Marc Evan Bonds approaches their relationship to those of Haydn in just such a way.[31] Bonds highlights those elements of Haydn's quartets to which Mozart reacted in a creative way, reinterpreting rather than simply copying his model. This is 'influence as transformation': 'Rather than focus on superficial similarities ... we should turn our attention to the process by which Mozart changes the models to which he alludes' (p. 377). 'Mozart ... used specific movements from Haydn's Op. 20 and Op. 33 as models but transformed those models so thoroughly as to create new works that on the surface, at least, appear to be without direct precedent' (p. 405).

Among Bonds' interesting, if at times controversial, discussions of such 'influence as transformation' is one that investigates the relationship between the finales of Haydn's Op. 20 no. 2 in C and Mozart's K.464. Haydn's finale is a superb fugue on four subjects in which invertible counterpoint plays a major role; Mozart's is not a strict fugue, though it picks up on some of Haydn's fugal devices, principally invertibility. While these movements' differences are more marked than their affinities they do share some common techniques. The affinities to which Bonds draws attention include chromaticism (both Haydn's and Mozart's opening themes feature four descending chromatic steps commencing on the dominant degree), thematic fragmentation (Mozart, bar 230ff.; compare Haydn at bars 83–7) and the appearance of the subject in inversion against itself (Mozart, bar 241; compare Haydn's bar 102ff.). A broader affinity is one of idiom: Bonds believes that Haydn's finale attempts a fusion of 'strict' and 'galant' styles and that Mozart acts likewise by incorporating fugal elements within an otherwise 'classic' frame of sonata form, post-galant harmonic structures and periodic phrasing. According to Bonds Mozart absorbed the salient features of Haydn's finale within his own, but proceeded from a 'complementary perspective. [Haydn's] Op. 20/2/iv opens with an initially contrapuntal texture but becomes increasingly homophonic; [Mozart's] K.464, by contrast, gives a hint of its contrapuntal nature in its opening measures but for the most part follows a trajectory that moves from homophony to polyphony, with the recapitulation and coda functioning as an apotheosis of invertible counterpoint' (p. 403).

Bonds' study highlights various ways in which a work can complement its predecessor, and suggests interesting avenues of enquiry for uncovering possible links between pieces never previously suspected. For example, it may be that the opening of K.387 (whose principal theme stresses, successively, tonic, dominant and tonic degrees, spanning an octave's space) was in some sense suggested by that of Haydn's Op. 33 no. 2 in E flat (beginning dominant, tonic, dominant – again spanning the octave), albeit in a rather different rhythmic disposition. Beyond this complementary pitch connection are some further similarities, such as the continuation beyond the first theme involving an extension of a cadential 'suffix' from the end of the phrase (bars 4^4–8 in Haydn; bars 5–10 in Mozart), followed by a restatement of the opening theme that incorporates some light contrapuntal exchange. If these features are indeed more than coincidental it may be that the cello's prominent chromatic-scale ascent which plays such a significant transitional role within Mozart's development (bars 72–80) is a 'complementary' reinterpretation of the chromatic central portion of Haydn's own development (beginning at bar 42) which outlines melodically decorated chromatic lines, both falling and rising, but principally in the highest part.[32]

Contemporary critiques

Mozart's 'Haydn' quartets continue to inspire fresh critical insights. Marc Evan Bonds' recent interpretations of these pieces suggest the possibility of both 'positive' and 'negative' influence within the tonal and formal conventions of the classic era.[33] Wye J. Allanbrook regards these works as 'a kind of composer's laboratory', leading her to a critique which combines two important eighteenth-century concepts, 'topic' and 'combinatorial' phrase-building as taught by Koch, and encourages us to listen afresh for ways in which their phrase-irregularities depart from the norm.[34] Konrad Küster usefully defines some of their technical procedures in relation to Haydn's and considers the important issue of Mozart's own compositional evolution during the mid-1780s. According to Küster, Mozart's 'technical and musical premisses altered for each of the quartets during the two years and more that passed between the composition of the first and last, so that in the end the set is more striking for the diversity of the six works than for representing variants of a uniform musical type'.[35]

Finally, I wish to turn to a recent critique of the Adagio of K.465 by Maynard Solomon which, in the spirit of this post-modern age, eschews several intervening generations of analytic methodology (Réti, Schenker) and returns to a hyper-textual interpretation of the passage's audacious harmonic language, rather reminiscent of Jahn:

> The opening bars ... immediately plunge into the center of symbiotic terror ... Here, Mozart has simulated the very process of creation, showing us the lineaments of chaos at the moment of its conversion into form ... Without knowing precisely where we are, we know that we are in an alien universe ... Reality has been defamiliarized, the uncanny has supplanted the commonplace. In this introduction, Mozart has simulated the transition from darkness to light, from the underworld to the surface, from the id to the ego. For, whatever our metaphoric frame, this music is ultimately about confinement and emergence. And now the Allegro theme emerges soaring and liberated...[36]

In his appeal to id and ego, Solomon also suggests a transition from classicism to romanticism, from the cool reason of Mozart's Enlightenment age to the fairy-tale domain of E. T. A. Hoffmann. Indeed, in Solomon's metaphors one detects an affinity with Hoffmann's writing: in *Kreisleriana* (1810) the latter speaks of Mozart as 'leading us deep into the realm of spirits. Dread lies all about us, but withholds its torments and becomes more an intimation of infinity.'[37]

In so far as these diverse contemporary critiques represent a multiplicity of approaches, they are manifestations also of one aspect of the post-modern critical condition which Richard Tarnas has identified as being characterised by 'a plurality of incompatible meanings. No interpretation of a text [including a musical text] can claim decisive authority because that which is being interpreted inevitably contains hidden contradictions that undermine its coherence. Hence all meaning is ultimately undecidable, and there is no "true" meaning ... The conflicts of subjective and objective testings, an acute awareness of the cultural parochialism and historical relativity of all knowledge ... and a pluralism bordering on distressing incoherence all contribute to the postmodern condition.'[38]

On a more positive note, the wealth of changing critical reactions provoked by these quartets during the two centuries since their composition celebrates their multivalent and seemingly inexhaustible layers of meaning. Each generation has found fresh revelations in this music, so 'universal' in its message that it allows each subsequent generation to reinterpret it according to the agenda of its own times, though without diminishing its essence. The 'Haydn' quartets continue to appeal to every time and to every taste, mediating effortlessly between melodic elegance and harmonic drama; solo display and gritty contrapuntal exchange; periodic dance and seamless fugue; 'high' and 'low' styles; simple and complex textures; formal convention and invention. One is reminded of a telling observation Mozart made to his father in 1782. Referring on 28 December that year to the three piano concertos K.413, K.414 and K.415, he remarked on the need for a freelance such as himself to appeal to different audiences simultaneously, and with regard to their musical education (or lack of one) and aesthetic expectations of a musical work: 'These concertos are a happy medium between what is too easy and too difficult ... There are passages here and there from which the connoisseurs alone can derive satisfaction; but these passages are written in such a way that the less learned cannot fail to be pleased, though without knowing why.' Mozart's comments could apply with equal force to his 'Haydn' quartets, whose manifold meanings we may continue to ponder, anticipating yet deeper pleasures, both in the searching and the finding.

Appendix

Mozart's dedication page (1785)

To my dear friend Haydn,

A father who had resolved to send his children out into the great world took it to be his duty to confide them to the protection and guidance of a very celebrated Man, especially when the latter by good fortune was at the same time his best Friend. Here they are then, O great Man and my dearest Friend, these six children of mine. They are, it is true, the fruit of a long and laborious endeavour, yet the hope inspired in me by several Friends that it may be at least partly compensated encourages me, and I flatter myself that this offspring will serve to afford me some solace one day. You yourself, dearest friend, told me of your satisfaction with them during your last Visit to this Capital. It is this indulgence above all which urges me to commend them to you and encourages me to hope that they will not seem to you altogether unworthy of your favour. May it therefore please you to receive them kindly and to be their Father, Guide and Friend! From this moment I resign to you all my rights in them, begging you however to look indulgently upon the defects which the partiality of a Father's eye may have concealed from me, and in spite of them to continue in your generous Friendship for him who so greatly values it, in expectation of which I am, with all my Heart, my dearest Friend, your most Sincere Friend

W. A. Mozart[1]

1 Translation from Deutsch, *Doc. Biog.*, 250.

Notes

Introduction

1 Three recent studies deserve special mention: Marc Evan Bonds, 'The Sincerest Form of Flattery? Mozart's "Haydn" Quartets and the Question of Influence', *Studi Musicale* 22 (1993), 365–409; Konrad Küster's 'Equal but Different: the Six "Haydn" Quartets' in his *Mozart: a Musical Biography*, trans. M. Whittall (Oxford, 1996); and Wye J. Allanbrook, '"To Serve the private pleasure": Expression and Form in the String Quartets', in S. Sadie, ed., *Wolfgang Amadè Mozart: Essays on his Life and Music* (Oxford, 1996), 132–60.

2 Alfred Einstein, *Mozart: his Character, his Work*, trans. A. Mendel and N. Broder (London, 1946), 183.

3 On the integration of enlightenment ideals into classic music, see Nicholas Till, *Mozart and the Enlightenment: Truth, Virtue and Beauty in Mozart's Operas* (London, 1991). Till notes (p.176) that 'in Mozart's use of counterpoint, the superabundance of individual melodic themes precludes their submergence and loss of identity within a despotic polyphonic texture; counterpoint becomes analogous to the interrelationship of free and equal individuals in society'.

4 Following the appearance of this first edition there were two subsequent impressions in *c.* 1787 and *c.* 1789 made from the original plates. For details see the *Kritische Berichte* to the *Neue Mozart Ausgabe* [*NMA*] VIII:20/1/ii, p. b/6.

5 Although K.458 was the fourth of the set to be completed, on 9 November 1784, it was begun in the summer of the previous year, possibly even before K.421; see Chapter 3. In the synopsis of the quartets given in Chapter 4 below, K.458 is examined as the third quartet of the series, following the printed order. According to Leopold Mozart, in a letter of 16 February 1785, K.458 belonged to a group of three 'new' quartets (the others being K.464 and K.465) 'which Wolfgang has added to the other three which we have already [K.387, K.421 and K.428]. The new ones are somewhat easier, but at the same time excellent compositions.' This is an

important stylistic observation. We may wonder, for instance, what Leopold considered 'easier' about the dense imitative (sometimes invertible) counterpoint in the finale of K.464, or the famous dissonant opening of K.465. Perhaps what he meant was that, for all their craftsmanship, the last three quartets are more overtly 'tuneful', more obviously periodic than their predecessors. They are all in major keys, avoiding the emotional turbulence of, for instance, the D minor quartet K.421, or the intellectual demands of the E flat quartet K.428. The ghostly chromatic unison figure in bars 1–4 is difficult to comprehend tonally at first hearing, and the fuller chromatic harmonisation it receives from bar 12, instead of asserting tonal stability, undermines it still further, referring sequentially to C minor, A flat, F minor before finally stabilising on a B flat pedal at bar 25. In its phraseology, too, this passage is far from straightforward (see Chapter 4). Compared to all this, the opening Allegros of K.458, K.464 and K.465 are, indeed, 'easier' to grasp. (This and all subsequent English translations are taken from Emily Anderson (trans and ed.), *The Letters of Mozart and his Family*, 3rd, rev. edn S. Sadie and F. Smart (London, 1983).)

6 For a different view, see Wolf-Dieter Seiffert, 'Mozarts "Haydn-Quartette": zum Quellenwert von Autograph und Erstausgabe unter besonderer Berücksichtigung des Finales aus KV 387', in *Studien zur Musikgeschichte: Eine Festschrift für Ludwig Finscher*, ed. A. Laubenthal and K. Kusan-Windweh (Kassel, 1995), 377–92.

7 *Wolfgang Amadeus Mozart: Complete String Quartets* (New York, 1970).

8 London, Zurich, Mainz and New York, 1930.

9 *W. A. Mozart: the Ten Celebrated String Quartets: 1st Authentic Edition in Score based on the Autographs in the British Museum and on Early Prints* (London, 1945).

1 Mozart's early quartets

1 Apparently only the first three movements were written at this stage, the Gavotte finale being composed later in 1773 or 1774. On Mozart's early string quartets, see Wolf-Dieter Seiffert, *Mozarts frühe Streichquartette* (Munich, 1992).

2 First performed 26 December 1771.

3 See Otto Erich Deutsch, *Mozart: a Documentary Biography*, trans. Eric Blom, Peter Branscombe and Jeremy Noble (London, 1990) (hereafter Deutsch, *Doc. Biog.*), 126–8 and 131–2, for details of the tests, citations and supporting testimonies.

4 As first suggested by Ludwig Finscher; see his 'Aspects of Mozart's Compositional Process in the Quartet Autographs: I. The Early Quartets, II. The Genesis of K.387', in *The String Quartets of Haydn, Mozart, and Beethoven: Studies of the Autograph Manuscripts*, Isham Library Papers III, ed. C. Wolff and R. Riggs (Cambridge, Mass., 1980), 121–53 (at p. 125) and his Facs. 5 (p. 139). The autograph is in the former collection of the Preußischer Staatsbibliothek, Berlin, now at the University of Tübingen.

5 A facsimile of this page is in *NMA* 18/i/1, p. xv.

6 For a facsimile, see *ibid.*, p. xvi.

7 For details, see Chapter 3.

8 See Cliff Eisen, *New Mozart Documents* (Stanford, 1991), no.129; *idem*, 'Contributions to a New Mozart Documentary Biography', *Journal of the American Musicological Society* 39 (1986), 625–6.

9 Einstein, *Mozart: his Character, his Work*, 75–8 (at p. 77). The influence of Haydn's quartets on those of Mozart is also assumed by Wyzewa and Saint-Foix.

10 For discussions of the supposed influence of Haydn's Op. 20 quartets on Mozart's see E. F. Schmid, 'Mozart and Haydn', in P. H. Lang (ed.), *The Creative World of Mozart* (New York, 1963), and Stanley Sadie, *Mozart* (London, 1965), 84. A recent attempt to sort out this problem is A. Peter Brown's 'Haydn and Mozart's 1773 Stay in Vienna: Weeding a Musicological Garden, *The Journal of Musicology* 10 (1992), 192–230. See also Walter Senn, 'Die Mozart-Überlieferung im Stift Heilig Kreuz zu Augsburg', *Neues Augsburger Mozart-Buch* (Augsburg, 1962), 333–68, which makes a case for Mozart having bought a set of playing parts of Haydn's Op. 17 quartets in Vienna in 1773, to which he made some handwritten additions. However, Mozart's additions appear not to have been made until the early 1780s. See Cliff Eisen, 'The Mozarts' Salzburg Music Library', in *Mozart Studies 2*, ed. C. Eisen (Oxford, forthcoming). I am grateful to Professor Eisen for sharing his findings with me before publication of his book.

2 Genesis of the 'Haydn' quartets

1 Mozart seems to be referring specifically to the violin and piano sonatas K.296 and K.376–80, published by Artaria in Vienna in 1781.

2 *Six Sonates pour Clavecin ou Forté Piano avec Accompagnement d'un Violon, dediées a Son Altesse électorale Madame l'Electrice Palatine par Wolfgang Amadeo Mozart fils* (Paris, 1778).

3 *Mozart's Thematic Catalogue: a Facsimile*, introduction and transcription by Albi Rosenthal and Alan Tyson (London: The British Library, 1990).

4 See *A Musical Pilgrimage. Being the Travel Diaries of Vincent & Mary Novello in the Year 1829*, ed. Rosemary Hughes (London, 1955), 112.

5 This is explicitly stated by Mozart in the published dedication of 1 September: 'Your good opinion encourages me to offer them to you and leads me to hope that you will not consider them wholly unworthy of your favour'.

6 Proudly reported by Leopold to his daughter in his letter of 16 February.

7 'The Sincerest Form of Flattery?' 370. Pleyel's Op. 2 quartets were published by Graeffer: *Sei Quartetti a due violini, viola e violoncello, composti e dedicate al celebrissimo estimatissimo fu suo maestro Giuseppe Haydn*.

8 Deutsch, *Doc. Biog.*, 252.

9 Mozart was perhaps referring to Pleyel's Op. 1 quartets, published by Graeffer in Vienna in 1783: *Sei Quartetti a due violini, viola e violoncello … opera I*.

10 A colour facsimile has been published: *Wolfgang Amadeus Mozart: The Six 'Haydn' String Quartets. Facsimile of the Autograph Manuscripts in the British Library Add. MS. 37763*, introduction by Alan Tyson, British Library Music Facsimiles 4 (London, 1985). The following discussion is greatly indebted to Tyson's work on Mozart's autographs. Tyson's original studies (which contain far more supporting commentary) are as follows: 'Mozart's "Haydn" Quartets: the Contribution of Paper Studies' and 'The Origins of Mozart's "Hunt" Quartet, K.458' (both reprinted in Tyson, *Mozart: Studies of the Autograph Scores* (Cambridge, Mass., 1987), 82–105).

11 See Deutsch, *Doc. Biog.*, 490–2, the 'Article of Agreement Between Constanze Mozart and Johann Anton André' (8 November 1799). The quartets listed on p. 492 include the six 'Haydn' quartets.

12 This was long thought to be lost. After many years in the Eastern Baptist Seminary, Philadelphia, the autograph was rediscovered in 1990, subsequently auctioned at Sotheby's, and is now available in a superb colour facsimile: *Wolfgang Amadeus Mozart: Fantasie c-Moll für Klavier KV 475 und Sonate c-Moll für Klavier KV 457: Faksimile Ausgabe nach dem Autograph in der Biblioteca Mozartiana Salzburg*, introduction by Wolfgang Plath and Wolfgang Rehm (Salzburg, 1991).

13 The rhetorical modes of address in dedications of musical publications have attracted little attention. A start is made in Marc Evan Bonds, 'The Sincerest Form of Flattery?' 366–71. That both Haydn and Mozart were

apparently familiar with rhetorical modes of writing is convincingly demonstrated by Elaine Sisman, *Haydn and the Classical Variation* (Cambridge, Mass., and London, 1993), 24–5, and *idem, Mozart: the 'Jupiter' Symphony* (Cambridge, 1993), 12–13.

14 Several other works were apparently left unfinished for a considerable period at about this time, among them the piano concertos K.449 and 488. See Tyson, *Mozart: Studies of the Autograph Scores*, 152–6, and his figures 11.3 and 11.4.

15 *Kritische Berichte Serie VIII: Kammermusik Werkgruppe 20: Streichquartette und Quartette mit einem Blasinstrument. Abteilung 1: Streichquartette Band 2*, ed. Ludwig Finscher and Wolf-Dieter Seiffert (Kassel, 1993).

16 For further details on the evolution of this finale see Ludwig Finscher, 'Aspects of Mozart's Compositional Process in the Quartet Autographs: II. The Genesis of K.387' and Marius Flothuis, 'A Close Reading of the Autographs of Mozart's Ten Late Quartets', in *The String Quartets of Haydn, Mozart, and Beethoven: Studies of the Autograph Manuscripts*, Isham Library Papers III, ed. C. Wolff and R. Riggs (Cambridge, Mass., 1980), 154–78.

17 Details are given on p. b/108 of the *Kritische Berichte* VIII/20/1/2. The sketches for K.464 appear on fol. 2v. The first is ten bars long, and opens with canonic imitations successively at the lower octave and at one bar's distance between first violin, second violin, viola and cello of a theme not actually found in the finale of K. 464, but of the same length and metric disposition in its first bar. A diplomatic transcription is given on p. b/166 of the *Kritische Berichte*. It is possible that this represents an early stage in the evolution of the theme itself, though the absence of clefs at the beginning of the system indicates that it cannot have been the initial draft. On this fragment, see also Ulrich Konrad, 'Neuentdecktes und wiedergefundenes Werkstattmaterial Wolfgang Amadeus Mozarts: erster Nachtrag zum Katalog der Skizzen und Entwürfe', in *Mozart-Jahrbuch* (1995), 20–2.

18 Printed in *NMA* VIII/20/1/3, App., no. 10. A reduced facsimile of the first folio is given in Alan Tyson's introduction to the British Library facsimile of the 'Haydn' quartets, p. x.

3 Steps to publication

1 As noted in letters of 16 and 21 February, 12 and 25–6 March, and 16 April 1785.

2 *Provinzialnachrichten Wien*, 5 March 1785, cited in Deutsch, *Doc. Biog.*,

238. A further advertisement for these concertos was placed in the *Wiener Realzeitung* on 29 March (Deutsch, *Doc. Biog.*, 242), this time coupled with the announcement of new symphonies by Haydn.

3 Deutsch, *Doc. Biog.*, 243.

4 *Trois Sonates pour le claveçin ou pianoforte ... composées par Mr. W. A. Mozart, dediées a son excellence Madame la Comtesse de Kobenzl ... Oeuvre VII* (Vienna, 1784), comprising the piano sonatas in B flat, K.333, and D, K. 284, and the violin sonata K.454. See A. Weinmann, 'Torricella' in *The New Grove* and his *Kataloge Anton Huberty (Wien) und Christoph Torricella* (Vienna, 1962).

5 *Wiener Zeitung*, 17 August 1785, cited in Deutsch, *Doc. Biog.*, 247.

6 *Wiener Zeitung*, 31 August 1785, cited in Deutsch, *Doc. Biog.*, 249.

7 These were published in 1786, originally by Torricella (though no copies of his edition are known to exist), and subsequently issued by Artaria, who bought some of Torricella's stock and engraving plates when that business was failing towards the end of 1786.

8 Cited in Deutsch, *Doc. Biog.*, 246. K.359, K.360 and K.455 were advertised in the *Wiener Zeitung* on 5 August 1786. Manuscript copies were advertised for sale by Lorenz Lausch as early as 31 August 1785, and by Johann Traeg on 14 September (both in *Wiener Zeitung*).

9 On Artaria, see Alexander Weinmann, *Vollständiges Verlagsverzeichnis Artaria & Comp.* (Vienna, 1952); 'Artaria', in *The New Grove*; and E. F. Schmid, 'Artaria', in *Musik in Geschichte und Gegenwart*. A useful digest of the firm's publishing activities is given in Peter Clive, *Mozart and his Circle* (London, 1993), 15–16.

10 The Op. 1 trios and the Op. 2 piano sonatas were published by Artaria in 1795 and 1796 respectively.

11 Sieber did bring out editions of the 'Haydn' quartets in 1791, 1792, 1801 and 1805–13; see *Kritische Berichte VIII/201/2*, pp. b/8–9.

12 Reprinted in Deutsch, *Doc. Biog.*, 252. An identical advertisement was placed in the *Wiener Realzeitung* on 18 September.

13 *Wiener Zeitung*, 10 September 1785; Deutsch, *Doc. Biog.*, 251.

14 *Wiener Zeitung*, 17 September; Deutsch, *Doc. Biog.*, 252.

15 Deutsch, *Doc. Biog.*, 252–3. The original source of this rebuttal has never been discovered. It was reported in Otto Jahn, *W. A. Mozart* (Leipzig, 1856), 355, and in the 3rd edition of *Köchel*, prepared by Alfred Einstein (1937), 233.

16 Deutsch, *Doc. Biog.*, 255. Some other dealers also sought to get in on the act, including the copyist and music-distributor, Lorenz Lausch, who advertised the Artaria prints for sale at the official price (6 fl. 30 kr.) at his

music shop within a month of their publication (Deutsch, *Doc. Biog.*, 254).

17 '[You ought to] do better with [my quartets] than you did with Mozart's (which indeed, I and still greater theorists consider to deserve the highest praise, but which because of their overwhelming and unrelenting artfulness are not to everyone's taste.)' See Eisen, *New Mozart Documents*, 54.

18 Letter of 2 December 1785.

4 The individual quartets: a synopsis

1 For a comprehensive survey of nineteenth-century writings on musical form see Ian Bent, *Analysis*, The New Grove Handbooks in Music (London, 1987), Chapter II; *idem*, 'Analytical Thinking in the First Half of the Nineteenth Century', in Edward Olleson (ed.), *Modern Musical Scholarship* (London, 1980), 151–66; and Ian Bent (ed.), *Music Analysis in the Nineteenth Century*, Vol. I: *Fugue, Form and Style*; Vol. II: *Hermeneutic Approaches* (Cambridge, 1994). The writings of eighteenth-century theorists are discussed in Leonard Ratner, *Classic Music, Expression, Form, Style* (New York, 1980), 217 ff. Sonata form is described in the following eighteenth-century treatises: Heinrich Christoph Koch, *Versuch einer Anleitung zur Composition* vol. II (Leipzig, 1787), 223; vol. III (Leipzig, 1793), 301 ff. and 341 ff.; Johann Georg Portmann, *Leichtes Lehrbuch der Harmonie, Composition, und des General-basses* (Darmstadt, 1789), 50; Georg Löhlein, *Clavierschüle* 5th edn. (Leipzig and Züllichau, 1791), 182 ff.; Francesco Galeazzi, *Elementi teorico-practici di Musica* vol. II (Rome, 1796), 251 ff.; August Kollmann, *An Essay on Practical Musical Composition* (London, 1799), 5.

2 An absorbing study of this subject has been made by Esther Cavett-Dunsby. See her 'Mozart's "Haydn" Quartets: Composing Up and Down Without Rules', *Journal of the Royal Musical Association* 113 (1988), 57–80.

3 Most probably *De rhythmopoeïa, oder von der Taktordnung* (Frankfurt and Leipzig, 1752) or *Grundregln zur Taktordnung insgemein* (Frankfurt and Leipzig, 1755).

4 Riepel, *Grundregln*, 36–71 *passim*.

5 At bars 13–16 and 65–70 the chromatic lines appear in imitative counterpoint, resulting in a 'polyphony' of alternating dynamics. These alternate *p, f, p* dynamics may, as Peter Williams suggests, derive from an aspect of contemporary violin pedagogy; see his chapter, 'Mozart's use of the Chromatic Fourth', in Peter Williams and R. Larry Todd (eds.), *Perspec-*

tives on Mozart Performance (Cambridge, 1991), at 209–10. It was not exclusively a bowing technique however, since Beethoven uses a similar type of alternation in the Andante of his G major Piano Sonata, Op. 14 no. 2 (bars 17–18, *et seq*). Alternating dynamics in a chromatic context are also found at bars 37–8 of the first movement of K.387, and bar 90 of K.428's Andante con moto.

6 Charles Rosen, *Sonata Forms* (New York and London, 1988), 108.

7 'Brahms the Progressive', in L. Stein and L. Black (trans. and ed.), *Style and Idea* (London, 1984) 415–16.

8 On the modifications to this recapitulation see Esther Cavett-Dunsby, 'Mozart's "Haydn" Quartets: Composing Up and Down Without Rules', 60–1.

9 Rosen, *Sonata Forms*, 112, 114.

10 James M. Baker, 'Chromaticism in Classical Music', in Christopher Hatch and David W. Bernstein (eds.), *Music Theory and the Exploration of the Past* (Chicago, 1993), 235.

11 Whereas sonata-form transitions often end on the dominant of the dominant, this one ends with a very prominent perfect cadence in the dominant itself.

12 The grace-note figure clearly refers to the rhythmic pattern at bar 40, though for some reason it is notated differently there.

13 *Grundregeln*, 36–71 *passim*.

14 *Fundamentals of Musical Composition*, ed. G Strang and L. Stein (London, 1967), 146–8.

15 Among other examples are the opening of the Fantasia in C minor, K.475, the Minuet of K.421 and the opening of Beethoven's 'Waldstein' Sonata, Op. 53. The introductory Adagio of K.465 is idiomatically similar to Mozart's C minor Fantasia (written later that same year, 1785) in that it contains melodic and harmonic gestures that evolve independently of a 'normal' tonal and periodic framework.

16 For an attempt to account for the prominent chromatic 'false relation' A–A flat at the beginning of the Adagio as a presaging of significant melodic and harmonic events later in the Allegro (and indeed, in subsequent movements of K.465) see Baker, 'Chromaticism in Classical Music', 286–94.

5 Some theoretical perspectives

1 See the letter of 11 June 1778, in which Leopold records his knowledge of theoretical works by a considerable number of eighteenth-century authors.

2 *Musikalischer Almanach auf das Jahr 1784*, 31–2. The translation is from Bonds, *Wordless Rhetoric: Musical Form and the Metaphor of the Oration* (Cambridge, Mass., 1991), 123–4. His section on Forkel's rhetorical interpretation of music (pp. 121–6) repays close study. Prior to this, he offers a rhetorical analysis of the first movement of K.465 (pp. 102, 112 and his Ex. 2.4) in which he pursues the rhetorical technique of *elaboratio* of a primary idea.

3 The other two were Memory (*memoria*) and Performance (*pronuntiatio*). All the relevant classical texts are listed in the Bibliography. The most important – *Ad Herrenium*, Quintilian's *Oratoria* and Cicero's *De Oratore* – were all published for the first time in Italy during the later fifteenth century, and remained essential (and oft-reprinted) educational aids in Europe until the first half of the nineteenth century.

4 It is worth recording that in the widely read compendium *Allgemeine Geschichte der schönen Künste* (Leipzig, 1771–4), Johann Georg Sulzer's discussion of the creative process outlines a sequence similar to Forkel's rhetorically derived model: *Erfindung* (Invention), *Entwurf* (Sketch), *Anlage* (Layout), *Form* (Form), *Plan* (Plan), *Anordnung* (Disposition) and *Ausarbeitung* (Elaboration). See Nancy Kovaleff Baker and Thomas Christensen (eds.), *Aesthetics and the Art of Musical Composition in the German Enlightenment* (Cambridge, 1995), 55–80.

5 *A Treatise on the Fundamental Principles of Violin Playing by Leopold Mozart*, trans. Edith Knocker (London, 1948; 2nd edn. 1951).

6 Gottsched's works were enormously important in mid-eighteenth-century German letters and were widely reprinted. Leopold owned the *Ausführliche Redekunst* (Augsburg, 1736) and *Grundlegung einer Deutschen Sprachkunst* (Augsburg, 1748). The importance of rhetoric in Leopold Mozart's education is argued further in John Irving, *Mozart's Piano Sonatas* (Cambridge, 1997), 106–8.

7 *Institutio*, III.iii.

8 *The Study of Counterpoint from Johann Joseph Fux's Gradus ad Parnassum*, trans. and ed. A. Mann (New York, 1965). Fig. 55 (p. 53) in Third Species and Fig. 82 (p. 64) in Fifth Species may be regarded as figured melodies in relation to the First Species original of Fig. 5 (p. 29). Mozart perhaps studied Fux's treatise – his father purchased a copy in 1746. Haydn explained to his biographer, Griesinger, that he had learned counterpoint from this text.

9 III, 26, reproduced in L. Ratner, *Classic Music: Expression, Form, and Style* (New York, 1980), 95.

10 See Elaine R. Sisman, 'Small and Expanded Forms: Koch's Model and Haydn's Music', *The Musical Quarterly* 68 (1982), 444–75.

11 Sisman, *Haydn and the Classical Variation* (Cambridge, Mass., 1993), Chapter 2.

12 IV.xxxi–xxxiv.

13 *Institutio*, VIII.vi.4–9 *passim*.

14 Most famously in his *Classic Music: Expression, Form and Style*. Wye J. Allanbrook's *Rhythmic Gesture in Mozart* (Chicago, 1983) is fundamental to any study of eighteenth-century topicality. A more recent discussion of topicality in late eighteenth-century music is in V. Kofi Agawu, *Playing with Signs: a Semiotic Interpretation of Classic Music* (Princeton, 1991), 26–50. Agawu offers a topically influenced analysis of the first movement of Mozart's C major Quintet, K.515, on pp. 80–99.

15 *Rhythmic Gesture*, 2.

16 The applicability of *Sturm und Drang* to Mozart's music has recently been questioned by Neal Zaslaw, principally on the grounds that most musical works alleged to exhibit *Sturm und Drang* characteristics predate the literary origins of that movement, namely Klinger's eponymous drama of 1776. See Zaslaw's *Mozart's Symphonies: Context, Performance Practice, Reception* (Oxford, 1989), 261–3. Nevertheless, it is a convenient term for such passages of overheated excitement.

17 Wye J. Allanbrook pursues the succession of topics in the second-subject group in K.428's Allegro non troppo. See '"To Serve the Private Pleasure"', 156 and Ex. 7.15.

18 See George Buelow, 'The Loci Topici and Affect in Late Baroque Music: Heinichen's Practical Demonstration', *The Music Review* 27 (1966), 161–76; 'Music, Rhetoric and the Concept of the Affections: a Selective Bibliography', *Notes* 30 (1973–4), 250–9.

19 Quoted in Deutsch, *Doc. Biog.*, 97–8.

20 The 'chasse' topic is quite obvious in, for instance, the finale of Mozart's fourth Horn Concerto K.495, in which the intervallic construction, featuring prominent tonic and dominant triads in the main melody, was to some degree dictated by the capability of the horn, and so was more closely allied with the original 'pure' characteristics of the 'chasse' as an open-air hunting call. Once defined, however, such 'chasse' characteristics could survive transplantation to other instruments and genres.

21 'The Chasse as a Musical Topic of the 18th Century', *Journal of the American Musicological Society* 6 (1953), 148–59.

22 Quintilian, *Institutio Oratoria*, VIII.vi.62–5. See also *Ad Herrenium*, IV.xxxii.

23 Quintilian, *Institutio*, IX.iii.54–5; *Ad Herrenium*, IV.xxv.

6 Reception of the 'Haydn' quartets

1 The quartets appeared in Series 14 (*Quartette für Streichinstrumente*) in Leipzig in 1881–2.

2 *Répertoire Internationale des Sources Musicales* [*RISM*] A/I/6, M6114, 6132.

3 *RISM* deest, A/I/6, M6145, 6147.

4 Sieber (Paris) published the quartets several times between 1791 and 1813. The earliest (*RISM* A/I/6, M6150) contains just K.465, K.387 and K.464, in that order; the remaining quartets appeared the following year (*RISM* A/I/6, M6140). Pleyel produced two editions, the first (*RISM* A/I/6, M.6139, M6151), of *c.* 1800, in two books of three (K.428, K.458, K.421; K.465, K.387, K.464), the second (not listed in *RISM*), of 1807–8, in three books of two (K.387, K.421; K.458, K.428; K.464, K.465).

5 *RISM* A/I/6, M6118.

6 *RISM* A/I/6, M6124.

7 The latter was published by André about 1824, an arrangement, by J. de Seyfried, of K.465's Andante (*RISM* A/I/6, M6227). Piano (either solo or duet) arrangements were made of the whole of K.387 (published by A. M. Schlesinger in Berlin, *c.* 1833, see the *Kritische Berichte* to *NMA* VIII:20/1/ii, p. Bb[8]); duet versions of the slow movement and finale variations of K.421 also appeared in editions published by Longman & Clementi (London, *c.*1800: *RISM* A/I/6, M6221) and P. C. Hilschner (Dresden, *RISM* A/I/6, M6220); no published piano arrangements of K.458, K.428, K.464 and K.465 are known to survive from the early nineteenth century.

8 *RISM* A/I/6, M6122, 6129, 6142, 6148, 6153.

9 K.387: Beethoven Archive, Bonn, sig. NE119 (part of the finale was detached from Beethoven's manuscript at some point and is now in the Pierpoint Morgan Library, New York (Mary Flagler Cary collection)). K.464: Stiftelser Musikkulturens Främjande, Stockholm (no call-mark). For a detailed investigation of the relationship between Beethoven's A major quartet Op. 18 no. 5 and Mozart's K.464 see Jeremy Yudkin, 'Beethoven's "Mozart" Quartet', *Journal of the American Musicological Society* 45 (1992), 30–73.

10 Translation from Nancy K. Baker, *Heinrich Christoph Koch: Introductory Essay on Composition – The Mechanical Rules of Melody, Sections 3 and 4* (New Haven and London, 1983), 197.

11 Reported in Leopold Mozart's letter of 3 November 1785 to Nannerl.

12 Quoted in Deutsch, *Doc. Biog.*, 290.

13 Among obvious illustrations are the contredanse elements in the finales of K.387 and K.465.

14 Another problem that contemporaries encountered was the quartets' harmonic idiom. According to Otto Jahn, *W. A. Mozart* (Leipzig, 1856–9; English translation, P. J. Townsend, London, 1882), III, 4, Prince Grassalkowitz had these works played by his musicians and, assuming that they were playing 'wrong' notes, checked the parts only to find that the dissonances were indeed specified, whereupon he tore the copies up in disgust! Perhaps the offending passage was the Adagio introduction of K.465 (see below). Thomas Attwood, Mozart's friend and pupil, presented a copy of these quartets to Giacomo Ferrari in late 1785, with the advice that Ferrari should not judge them until he had heard them several times. Ferrari and 'various dilettanti and teachers' could play only 'the slow movements, and even these only with difficulty'. See C. Eisen, *New Mozart Documents* (Stanford, 1991), p. 81.

15 3 vols. (Paris, 1806). The sections devoted to Mozart's quartet are I, 307–82; II, 387–403; and III, 109–56 (an extended musical example).

16 I, 371 (author's translation). The text appended to Momigny's annotated score in volume III of the treatise begins 'Ah! quand tu fais mon déplaisir, ingrat, je veux me plaindre, et non pas t'attendrir'.

17 *La Revue musicale* series 1, vol. 5 (July 1829), 601–6. On this controversy, see J. A. Vertrees, 'Mozart's String Quartet K.465: the History of a Controversy', *Current Musicology* 17 (1974), 96–114.

18 *La Revue musicale* series 1, vol. 6 (August 1829), 25–34.

19 *La Revue musicale* series 2, vol. 8 (July 1830), 321–8 ('Nouvelles discussions sur l'introduction d'un quatuor de Mozart').

20 *Cäcilia* 14 (1832), 1–49.

21 Taken from the translated summary of Sarti's *Esame acustico fatto sopra due frammenti di Mozart* given in the *Allgemeine musikalische Zeitung* 34 (1832), 373. Sarti believed this passage of Mozart's quartet to be 'barbarous'.

22 Leipzig and Halle, 1791; 4th, rev. edn. 1824.

23 *The Harmonicon*, 10 (1832), 243–6, under the title, 'Sarti *versus* Mozart'. The other 'fragment' was the opening of K.421.

24 'Sarti *versus* Mozart', 246.

25 *W. A. Mozart*, III, 10, 12.

26 *Ibid.*, 3.

27 Hans Keller, 'The Chamber Music', in H. C. Robbins Landon and D. Mitchell (eds.), *The Mozart Companion* (London, 1956), 90–1, 116.

28 *Ibid.*, 103–4.

29 Stanley Sadie, *Mozart* (London, 1965), 88. In Sadie's later article on Mozart for *The New Grove* (1980) he notes '[that Mozart] sought to emulate Haydn's op. 33 ... can scarcely be doubted. The debt to Haydn lies rather in the general approach to quartet style than in ... specific resemblances ... though [these] are sufficiently marked to leave no doubt about Mozart's knowledge of the Haydn works or his interest, conscious or no, in vying with them.'

30 Alfred Einstein, *Mozart: his Character, his Work*, 175–8; Theodore de Wyzewa and Georges de Saint-Foix, *Wolfgang Amédée Mozart: sa vie musicale et son œuvre*, 5 vols. (Paris, 1912–46), II, 55–82.

31 Marc Evan Bonds, 'The Sincerest Form of Flattery?' 365–409.

32 For a recent discussion of this type of 'influence as transformation', using techniques derived from literary criticism (specifically Harold Bloom's *The Anxiety of Influence: a Theory of Poetry* (Oxford, 1973)), see Kevin Korsyn, 'Towards a New Poetics of Musical Influence', *Music Analysis* 10 (1991), 3–72; and Susan Youens, 'Schubert, Mahler and the Weight of the Past: "Lieder eines fahrenden Gesellen" and "Winterreise"', *Music and Letters* 67 (1986), 256–68.

33 'The Sincerest Form of Flattery?' 365–409.

34 '"To Serve the Private Pleasure"', 133.

35 'Equal but Different: the Six "Haydn" Quartets', in his *Mozart: a Musical Biography* (Oxford, 1996), 194.

36 Maynard Solomon, *Mozart: a Life* (London, 1995), 200.

37 See David Charlton (ed.), *E. T. A. Hoffmann's Musical Writings: Kreisleriana, the Poet and the Composer, Music Criticism*, trans. Martyn Clarke (Cambridge, 1989), 99.

38 Richard Tarnas, *The Passion of the Western Mind* (London, 1991), 399, 398.

Select bibliography

The quartets: prints and manuscripts

Wolfgang Amadeus Mozart: Neue Ausgabe Sämtliche Werke Serie VIII: Kammermusik Werkgruppe 20: Streichquartette und Quartette mit einem Blasinstrument. Abteilung 1: Streichquartette Band 2, ed. Karl Heinz Füssl, Wolfgang Plath and Wolfgang Rehm (Kassel, etc., 1966).

Wolfgang Amadeus Mozart: Kritische Berichte Serie VIII: Kammermusik Werkgruppe 20: Streichquartette und Quartette mit einem Blasinstrument. Abteilung 1: Streichquartette Band 2, ed. Ludwig Finscher and Wolf-Dieter Seiffert (Kassel, 1993).

Wolfgang Amadeus Mozart: the Six 'Haydn' String Quartets. Facsimile of the Autograph Manuscripts in the British Library Add. MS. 37763, introduction by Alan Tyson, British Library Music Facsimiles IV (London, 1985).

Books and articles

Allanbrook, Wye J. '"To Serve the Private Pleasure": Expression and Form in the String Quartets', in Stanley Sadie (ed.), *Wolfgang Amadè Mozart: Essays on his Life and Music* (Oxford, 1996), 132–60.

Anderson, Emily (trans and ed.). *The Letters of Mozart and his Family*, 3rd, rev. edn S. Sadie and F. Smart (London, 1983).

Aristotle. *The 'Art' of Rhetoric*, trans. John Henry Freese, Loeb Classical Library no. 193 (Cambridge, Mass., and London, 1926, rep. 1991).

Bach, C. P. E. *Versuch über die wahre Art das Clavier zu spielen* (Berlin, 1753). English trans. W. J. Mitchell as *C. P. E. Bach: Essay on the True Art of Playing Keyboard Instruments* (London, 1949).

Baker, Nancy Kovaleff and Thomas Christensen (ed. and trans.). *Aesthetics and the Art of Musical Composition in the German Enlightenment: Selected Writings of Johann Georg Sulzer and Heinrich Christoph Koch* (Cambridge, 1995).

Bauer, Wilhelm, and Otto E. Deutsch (eds.). *Wolfgang Amadeus Mozart, Briefe und Aufzeichnungen* (Salzburg, 1962–75).

Bonds, Marc E. *Wordless Rhetoric: Musical Form and the Metaphor of the Oration* (Cambridge, Mass., 1991).

'The Sincerest Form of Flattery? Mozart's "Haydn" Quartets and the Question of Influence', in *Studi Musicali* 22 (1993), 365–409.

Buelow, George. 'The Concept of "Melodielehre": a Key to Classic Style', in *Mozart Jahrbuch* (1978–9), 182–95.

'The Loci Topici and Affect in Late Baroque Music: Heinichen's Practical Demonstration', *The Music Review* 27 (1966), 161–76.

'Music, Rhetoric and the Concept of the Affections: a Selective Bibliography', *Notes* 30 (1973–4), 250–9.

Cavett-Dunsby, Esther. *Mozart's Variations Reconsidered: Four Case Studies (K.613, K.501 and the Finales of K.421 (417b) and K.491)* (New York and London, 1989).

'Mozart's "Haydn" Quartets: Composing Up and Down without Rules', *Journal of the Royal Musical Association* 113 (1988), 57–80.

[pseudo-Cicero]. *Ad Herrenium*, trans. H. Caplan, Loeb Classical Library no. 403 (Cambridge, Mass., and London, 1954, rep. 1989).

Cicero. *De Inventione*, trans. H. M. Hubbell, Loeb Classical Library no. 386 (Cambridge, Mass., and London, 1949, rep. 1976).

De Oratore, trans. E. W. Sutton and H. Rackham, Loeb Classical Library no. 348 (Cambridge, Mass., and London, 1942, rep. 1988).

Clive, Peter. *Mozart and his Circle* (London, 1993).

Deutsch, Otto E. *Mozart: a Documentary Biography*, trans. E. Blom, P. Branscombe and J. Noble (London, 1965) [Deutsch, *Doc. Biog.*].

Devriès, Anik, and François Lesure. *Dictionnaire des Editeurs de Musique français* (Geneva, 1979).

Downs, Philip G. *Classical Music: the Era of Haydn, Mozart and Beethoven* (New York and London, 1992), 139.

Einstein, Alfred. *Mozart: his Character, his Work*, trans. A. Mendel and N. Broder (London, 1946).

Eisen, Cliff. *New Mozart Documents* (Stanford, 1991).

Eisen, Cliff (ed.). *Mozart Studies* (Oxford, 1991).

Mozart Studies 2 (Oxford, forthcoming).

Feder, Georg. 'Haydn', *The New Grove Dictionary of Music and Musicians* (London, 1980).

Finscher, Ludwig. 'Aspects of Mozart's Compositional Process in the Quartet Autographs: I. The Early Quartets, II. The Genesis of K.387', in *The String Quartets of Haydn, Mozart, and Beethoven: Studies of the*

Autograph Manuscripts, Isham Library Papers III, ed. Christoph Wolff and Robert Riggs (Cambridge, Mass., 1980), 121–53.

Flothuis, Marius. 'A Close Reading of the Autographs of Mozart's Ten Late Quartets', in *The String Quartets of Haydn, Mozart, and Beethoven: Studies of the Autograph Manuscripts*, Isham Library Papers III, ed. Christoph Wolff and Robert Riggs (Cambridge, Mass., 1980), 154–78.

Forkel, Johann Nikolaus. *Allgemeine Geschichte der Musik*, 2 vols. (Leipzig, 1788–1801).

Fux, Johann Joseph. *Gradus ad Parnassum* (Vienna, 1725). English trans. A. Mann (ed.), *The Study of Counterpoint from Johann Joseph Fux's Gradus ad Parnassum* (New York, 1965).

Irving, John. *Mozart's Piano Sonatas: Contexts, Sources, Style* (Cambridge, 1997).

Jahn, Otto. *W. A. Mozart* (Leipzig, 1856).

Keller, Hans. 'The Chamber Music', in H. C. Robbins Landon and D. Mitchell (eds.) *The Mozart Companion* (London, 1956), 90–137.

Kirnberger, Johann. *Die Kunst des reinen Satzes in der Musik* (Berlin, 1771–9).

Koch, Heinrich Christoph. *Versuch einer Anleitung zur Composition* (Leipzig, 1782–93).

Musikalisches Lexicon (Frankfurt-am-Main, 1802).

Kollmann, August F. C. *An Essay on Practical Musical Composition* (London, 1799).

Küster, Konrad. *Mozart: a Musical Biography*, trans. M. Whittall (Oxford, 1996)

Marpurg, Friedrich. *Handbuch bey dem Generalbasse und der Composition* (Berlin, 1755).

Mattheson, Johann. *Der vollkommene Capellmeister* (Hamburg, 1739).

Johann Matthesons General-Bass-Schule (Hamburg, 1731).

Kern melodischer Wissenschaft (Hamburg, 1737).

Momigny, J. J. de. *Cours complet d'Harmonie et de Composition* (Paris, 1806).

Mozart Eigenhändiges Werkverzeichnis Faksimile. Introduction and translation by A. Rosenthal and A. Tyson (Kassel, 1991).

Niemetschek, F. X. *Leben des k.k. Kapellmeisters Wolfgang Gottlieb Mozart nach Originalquellen beschrieben* (Prague, 1797).

Portmann, Johann G. *Leichtes Lehrbuch der Harmonie, Composition, und des Generalbasses* (Darmstadt, 1789).

Quintilian. *Institutio Oratoria*, trans. H. E. Butler (Cambridge, Mass., and London, 1921, rep. 1986).

Ratner, Leonard. *Classic Music: Expression, Form, and Style* (New York, 1980).

Riepel, Josef. *Anfangsgründe zur musikalischen Setzkunst I: De Rhythmopoeïa oder von der Tactordnung* (Augsburg, 1752; Regensburg, 1754).

Grundregeln zur Tonordnung insgemein (Frankfurt and Leipzig, 1755).

Ringer, Alexander. 'The Chasse as a Musical Topic of the 18th Century', *Journal of the American Musicological Society* 6 (1953), 148–59.

Rosen, Charles. *The Classical Style: Haydn, Mozart, Beethoven* (London, 1971).

Sonata Forms, rev. edn (New York and London, 1988).

Rousseau, Jean-Jacques. *Dictionnaire de Musique* (Paris, 1768).

Sadie, Stanley. 'Mozart', *The New Grove Dictionary of Music and Musicians* (London, 1980).

Mozart (London, 1965).

Schoenberg, Arnold. *Fundamentals of Musical Composition*, ed. G. Strang and L. Stein (London, 1967).

'Brahms the Progressive', in L. Stein and L. Black (trans. and ed.), *Style and Idea*, rev. edn (London, 1984), 398–441.

Seiffert, Wolf-Dieter. *Mozarts frühe Streichquartette* (Munich, 1992).

Sisman, Elaine R. *Haydn and the Classical Variation* (Cambridge, Mass., 1993).

Mozart: the 'Jupiter' Symphony (Cambridge, 1993).

Solomon, Maynard. *Mozart: a Life* (London, 1995).

Sutcliffe, W. Dean. *Haydn String Quartets, Op. 50* (Cambridge, 1992).

Till, Nicholas. *Mozart and the Enlightenment: Truth, Virtue and Beauty in Mozart's Operas* (London, 1991).

Tyson, Alan. *Mozart: Studies of the Autograph Scores* (Cambridge, Mass., 1987).

'Mozart's "Haydn" Quartets: the Contribution of Paper Studies', in *The String Quartets of Haydn, Mozart, and Beethoven: Studies of the Autograph Manuscripts*, Isham Library Papers III, ed. Christoph Wolff and Robert Riggs (Cambridge, Mass., 1980), 179–90.

'The Origins of Mozart's "Hunt" Quartet, K.458', in *Music and Bibliography: Essays in Honour of Alec Hyatt King*, ed. O. Neighbour (London, 1980), 132–48.

Weinmann, Alexander. *Vollständiges Verlagsverzeichnis Artaria & Comp.* (Vienna, 1952).

Kataloge Anton Huberty (Wien) und Christoph Torricella (Vienna, 1962).

'Artaria', *The New Grove Dictionary of Music and Musicians* (London, 1980).

'Torricella', *The New Grove Dictionary of Music and Musicians* (London, 1980).

'Traeg', *The New Grove Dictionary of Music and Musicians* (London, 1980).

Verlagsverzeichnis Johann Traeg (und Sohn), 2nd, rev. edn (Vienna, 1973).

Wolff, Christoph. 'Creative Exuberance vs. Critical Choice: Thoughts on Mozart's Quartet Fragments', in *The String Quartets of Haydn, Mozart, and Beethoven: Studies of the Autograph Manuscripts*, (Cambridge, Mass., 1980), Isham Library Papers III, ed. Christoph Wolff and Robert Riggs, 191–210.

Yudkin, Jeremy. 'Beethoven's "Mozart" Quartet', *Journal of the American Musicological Society* 45 (1992), 30–73.

Index

Index

Operas:
Ascanio in Alba, 5
Die Entführung aus dem Serail, 19
Lucio Silla, 5
Mitridate, ré di Ponto, 5
Piano concertos:
  K.413–15, 12, 19, 20, 84
  K.453, 20
Piano sonata, K.311, 32
Piano variations, K.265, K.359, K.360,
  K.398, K.455, 20
Serenade, K.203, 43
String quartets:
  K.80, 5, 8
  K.155–60, 1, 5–11 *passim*
  K.168–73, 1, 5–11 *passim*, 22
  K.387, 1, 2, 12, 13, 15, 16, 18, 22,
    25–33, 50, 75, 79–80, 81, 87
  K.421, 1, 2, 3, 13, 14, 15, 16, 22, 26,
    33–7, 53, 63, 75, 76, 80, 87, 93
  K.428, 1, 2, 3, 10, 11, 13, 14, 16, 22,
    26, 37–44, 63, 65, 66, 68, 75, 87
  K.458, 1, 2, 3, 4, 10, 13, 15, 16, 17,
    22, 26, 44–9, 65, 66, 68–72, 87
  K.464, 1, 3, 14, 15, 16, 22, 26, 49–54,
    63–4, 67, 68, 75, 81, 87, 90
  K.465, 1, 2, 3, 10, 13, 15, 16, 22, 26,
    54–60, 63, 65, 66, 68, 75, 77–8, 80,
    82–3, 87
Symphonies:
  K.183, 8
  K.385, 21
  K.550, 60
Trio, K.254, 20
Violin sonatas:
  K.296, 21
  K.301–06, 12
  K.376–80, 21

Novello, M., 13
Novello, V., 13

Plath, W., 8
Pleyel, I., 13, 73
Plowden, C. H. C., 14
Plowden, H., 14

Quintilian, 62, 63, 67

rhetoric, 61–8 *passim*
Riepel, J., 27–8, 46, 55
Rosen, C., 30, 36
Rousseau, J-J., 2

Sadie, S., 98
Sammartini, G. B., 5, 6, 7
Sarti, G., 77
Schoenberg, A., 51
Sieber, J. G., 12, 21, 73
Sisman, E., 67
Solomon, M., 82–3
Stumpff, J. A., 14
Sukowaty, W., 19

Tarnas, R., 83
Tinti, Barons, 13
topics, 68–72
Torricella, C., 1, 19, 20, 22
Traeg, J., 20, 73
Trattner, T., 21
Türk, D. G., 77
Tyson, A., 14

Vanhal, J., 21

Weber, G., 77